MARKETPLACE SHIFT

Activating Christians in the Workplace for Kingdom Expansion

Silas A. Achu

MARKETPLACE SHIFT

Activating Christians in the Workplace for Kingdom Expansion

© Copyright 2020 – Silas A. Achu/KMHP
ISBN 978-163587671-0

Produced and Published by
Kingdom Media House Publishing (KMHP)
Telephone/Whatsapp: +8617880217320

All rights reserved. No part of this book may be copied or reprinted for commercial gain or profit. The use of short quotations or occasional page copying for personal or group study is permitted and encouraged. Permission will be granted upon request.

Unless otherwise identified, Scripture quotations are from the New King James Version. Copyright 1982 by Thomas Nelson, Inc. Used by permission. All rights reserved. All emphasis within scripture quotations is the author's own.

Please note that the publishing style capitalizes certain pronouns in Scripture that refer to the Father, Son, and Holy Spirit, and may differ from some publishers' styles.

Take note that the name satan and related names are not capitalized. We choose not to acknowledge him, even to the point of violating grammatical rules.

For more information, please contact silasachu@outlook.com

Cover Design: A.DA Creative
Printed in China

ENDORSEMENTS

THERE is no person I know personally who is qualified to write a book on the marketplace than my friend Silas. I have had the privilege of working with him in the marketplace and to see the transformation he has brought to the workplace. This book will give you proven concepts that will transform your life and equip you to step into your purpose and destiny in the marketplace.

I encourage you to read this book slowly and meditatively so that these truths can sink deep into your subconscious mind and bring transformation in your life."

___**Wango Boris, Pastor**
Senior Leader, Bethel Atlanta Cameroon
Buea, Cameroon

"These are the kind of books you study and your view about being the light to the world, and the salt to the Earth is made so clear. I recommend it as a must-read book if we have a passion to bring about Kingdom expansion here on Earth as Christians"

___**Bonam Lessly, Reverend**
Senior Leader, Glory Streams Ministries
Buea, Cameroon

"This is a beautiful piece. I am excited to know that God has inspired Silas with such great insights that demystify some of the hidden truths about Christianity and the marketplace. God is raising Christians in every area of society today so they can use their positions to positively influence the decisions of nations.

I greatly recommend this book as it is going to change your mind-set dramatically. We need more revolutionary writers like Silas. I am persuaded God is going to use this writer to bring that mindset change that we have been praying and hoping for. God richly bless you as you read."

___**Christel Franklin, Evangelist**
Founder, Deborah Bread of Women Initiative
Toronto, Canada

"This book is filled with incredible tactical insight for Christians who are grappling to leave a positive contribution to humanity (the marketplace) and still stand firm in their walk with God. It is time to challenge yesterday's thinking and change how we get things done as Christian professionals and business people.

The 5 paradigm shifts raised in this piece will orchestrate a novel set of marketplace ministers who will advance the Kingdom in the marketplace"

___**Javnyuy Joybert, Mr. Remarkable**
Head Trainer, Lead Consultant & CEO, COSDEF Group Ltd
Yaoundé, Cameroon

This book has completely transformed my way of looking at life as a Christian. It is an eye-opener. Every pastor needs a copy and every Christian needs one as well. Serious kingdom business persons should make this book a must-read for their staff.

To be an effective 21st century Christian in the marketplace, you need the roadmap put out in this book. To be a Christian operating with the kingdom mind-set of dominion, taking over every area of influence for God, this book is what you need.

___**Tem Martin, Journalist**
Author of Developing the Entrepreneur's Mindset Author/ Speaker/Entrepreneur, Nigeria

"The great commission Jesus gave states "Go therefore and make disciples in all nations…." In this commission, the area in which God calls the Christian to operate and build disciples is ALL NATIONS; not churches. This means the work of the Christian is not limited to the church. In fact, most of the work in achieving the great commission is not in the church but in the marketplace.

Anyone who is concerned with fulfilling the great commission and making sure that the will of God is done on earth as it is in heaven, will find Marketplace Shift to be a great tool.

I recommend this book to all Christians; for a change in paradigm so that we can definitely be the salt of the earth and light of the world."

___**Godlove NJISONG, Life Coach**
Founder, GoMAD Network
Douala, Cameroon

In Marketplace Shift, Pastor Silas redefines the role of the believer vis-a-vis societal impact. He equally examines the kingdom expectations and requirements for dominion in the real sense.

The book ushers a crystal perspective on the succinct transformation possible when believers correctly invade the marketplace and equally throws the downturns if believers do not. This is a book for this present dispensation.

___**Rochie Osvalin, Pastor & Gospel Artist**
Lead Pastor, Christland Ministries Buea
Marketing and Sales Manager, Cassvita Cameroon
CEO, Worship Nation, Network1000

This book is a portable reformation manual. If you have a calling to change society or any sphere of influence, this is your starting point. This book will equip you from the foundations of God's Kingdom to all the other misunderstood departments or concepts that flow from it.

Silas has tackled some of the most misunderstood concepts in church and our world today in a very practical and 'non-Christianese' language. He practically challenges conventional thought patterns. This book will teach you how to think!

___**Kingsley Ndive, Pastor**
Resident Pastor, Bethel Atlanta Cameroon
Buea, Cameroon

"This is a book for anybody who wants to be at the center of what God is doing in our generation. I must warn you that this book will challenge you to think out of the box to figure out how to put new wine into a new wineskin.

If you are still wondering why we need to shift to a kingdom mind-set, consider the following as succinctly stated by Pastor Silas Achu, "The Kingdom of God only grows when the church imparts its values to the kingdoms of this world."

This is a must-read book for anybody who wants to be involved in advancing the Kingdom of God on earth, and I strongly recommend it."

___**Dr. Eric Tangumonkem, Ph.D**
President, IEM Approach LLC, USA
Author, Speaker, Coach

This book will teach you about the relevance and importance of marketplace ministry and ignite you to listen to the daily whispers of the Lord at your work. I encourage you to meditatively study and understand the concepts in this book; it will change your life and view towards ministry. I believe there is a shift into the marketplace for effective transformation of our world and this piece of work is one of many that will propel us into such a shift. Let the marketplace ministers arise as they read this piece.

Silas is one of the best I know in the marketplace who is not just speaking words but is actively living in the fullness of his call as a marketplace minister. Let his words impart and ignite you to arise."

___**Ekpombang Bessie Nchenge**
Director, BACSSM
Director, Transformation Centre
Bethel Atlanta Cameroon
Buea, Cameroon

"Silas has a strong apostolic anointing for kingdom business and this book Marketplace Shift is the road map or guidebook for many with a similar calling who shy away from their call. Following the principles laid down in this book will inspire to action the reader and provoke a strong apostolic movement of kingdom businesspersons who will transform the economy of the nations."

___**John Ayuk-Nchong Nchong Mbeng, Pastor**
Pastor, Redeemed Christian Church of God (RCCG)
CEO, Christian Transformation Initiative
Founder, Bornstar Impact Group
Yaoundé, Cameroon

DEDICATION

I DEDICATE this book to Christians around the world who have devoted their lives to transform their workplaces and communities by being the salt and the light in the darkness; through the power of the gospel.

May your light so shine that all men may see it and give glory to the Father in Heaven.

ACKNOWLEDGEMENT

TO write a book of this magnitude requires the effort and input of many people.

I will like to first acknowledge and express my great gratitude to the Father, for the grace, inspiration, and wisdom to successfully embark on the project of writing this book. This has not been an easy journey; however, I could clearly see the hand of God at work, enabling me to successfully complete this work. This book is first and foremost for the Father's glory and I give Him all praise.

I will like to express my sincere thanks to my most lovely and dear wife, Vivian; my ever-present help in all things. Thank you for your tireless sacrifices and devotion to me; thank you for the constant encouragement to finish this work, despite the many setbacks and challenges we had to go through.

To embark on a spiritual work like this will not be possible without the backing and support of a strong cover of prayer, counsel, and spiritual oversight. I have had so much support from my Bethel Family through Dr Sherri Lewis, Ps Wango Boris, Ps Bessie; special thanks to Ps. Willy Herbert and his wife Euphrasia Egbe of Glory Stairway Church, Buea, for their support and encouragement, both spiritually and materially.

From the time I came into this world until this very day, I have never stopped experiencing the love and support of my parents. I will like to especially thank my mum, Mama Theresia Bih Achu for her sacrifices, fasting, and prayers for me. This work is a product of the seeds she sowed in me in so many ways over the years. I will also like to acknowledge the immense efforts of my late father, Pa Isaac Achu Fomukong (of blessed memory) for the disciplines and strong foundations he embedded in me from my childhood. And in the same light, I like to express my gratitude to my siblings; Irene, Cynthia, Terence, Sheila, Beatrice, and Felicita. Thank you for your continuous support towards my sometimes complicated ministry and walk with the Lord.

There is this special group of people I met in 2019 in South Africa; coming from over 30 nations. Space won't permit me to list all their names here but I sincerely want to appreciate the ALICT Class of 2019. My life was forever changed when I met this group of wonderful Kingdom Ambassadors and that experience only made my commitment to this project even stronger. I cannot forget to give very special thanks to my brother Mensah Bodylawson, who did the very first and most comprehensive editing of this work. Thank you so much for your input which greatly helped to simplify the presentation of the truths shared in this book.

Finally, I give special thanks to my Bethel church family. Everything I share in this book has its roots in the culture and values of Bethel and the things I have learned here.

CONTENTS

Endorsements iii

Dedication x

Acknowledgement xi

Foreword xv

Introduction 19

Chapter One 25
    PARADIGM SHIFT

Chapter Two 41
    GOSPEL SHIFT

Chapter Three 63
    MINISTRY SHIFT

Chapter Four 93
    WORSHIP SHIFT

Chapter Five 117
    CULTURE SHIFT

Chapter Six 149
    CHURCH SHIFT

Chapter Seven 179
    KINGS AND PRIESTS

End Notes 199

Bibliography 202

About the Author 208

Other Books 210

FOREWORD

IT has been projected that the largest harvest of souls in the coming seasons will not come from ministry in the church, as we've known it, but from Christians in the marketplace, sharing the gospel in everyday life. That was Jesus' original plan. Before He ascended, He gave power to His Apostles and told them to disciple nations. (Matt. 28:28) That was His Kingdom mandate for transforming the world, and it hasn't changed.

What has changed is the church and our approach to sharing the gospel. Our approach to discipling nations and bringing about cultural transformation has deteriorated to a state, not at all reflective of Jesus' mandate. The Apostles were described as, "Those that have turned the world upside down." One of the greatest accusations against them was that they were actively engaged in changing the world, so much so that they were seen as a threat to the status quo of the Roman Empire.

I wonder how history will describe the church that we've been for the last two centuries. *"Those that turned inward and hid in the church, only affecting one another?" "Those that turned their back in judgment on the world, condemning it to hell by not affecting the change they were uniquely qualified and equipped to bring about?"*

God forbid! It's time for the church to return to the initial mandate given by Christ. It's time for us to disciple nations.

It's time for us to become, once again, those that bring about cultural transformation and turn the world upside down!

Marketplace Shift is a powerful tool toward that end. It is an exhaustive, comprehensive, and forensic guidebook in producing a new breed of marketplace ministers Christians who carry the Gospel of the Kingdom in their everyday life, into the workplace and wherever they go.

Silas Achu is highly qualified to teach on this subject. I first met him in 2010, when he was a first-year student in our Bethel Atlanta Cameroon School of Supernatural Ministry. He devoured the foundational teachings including, The Message of the Kingdom, Kingdom Citizenship, Purpose and Destiny, Identity, and particularly the 7 Mountains of Influence. Over the last ten years, I've seen few students internalize and personalize these core messages with the depth of passion, fire, and personal responsibility that he has. He became the message of the Kingdom and cultural transformation.

I've also watched his frustration in attempting to engage church leaders who didn't agree with his views on cultural transformation. I was concerned that perhaps the fire might die as he was discouraged from excelling in the marketplace and marketplace ministry. Recently though, God has rekindled that fire and the cultural transformer is vibrantly alive and ready to engage in the epic battle Kingdom Christians wage in discipling nations.

He is uniquely qualified to teach not only because of his expertise on the subject, and his passion for marketplace transformation, but even more so because he's fought the personal battle of championing the cause of this teaching in a non- accepting environment. Through it all, he's stayed true to his core values as a world-changing, marketplace revivalist.

As an international best-selling author, I'm impressed at how excellently the book is written and the wealth and depth of information shared. As a Kingdom leader and apostolic strategist, I am excited about the potential impact of this book on the body of Christ. It will be a must-read in our 2nd and 3rd deployment years in our schools of ministry and Kingdom Leadership Academy.

As Silas' spiritual mother, I read this book with so much pride almost in tears seeing the passionate Kingdom revivalist live again to arise and fulfil the call on his life.

I bless you as you read and allow for the five paradigm shifts covered in the book to transform your perspective so you can be an effective marketplace minister. Let's transform culture, change the world, and disciple nations!

Dr. Sherri Lewis
International Bestselling Author
Founder & Director, Bethel Atlanta Africa
Kenya, Cameroon, USA

INTRODUCTION

IN this book, there are two words I need to define early on: *marketplace* and *workplace*.

Marketplace: The world of commercial activity where goods and services are bought and sold.

Workplace: A place where work is done.

When I refer to the workplace, I am referring the kind of work that is done primarily in the world of commercial activity where goods and services are bought and sold, and which is called the marketplace. So as you read this book, you will see me use the words workplace and marketplace interchangeably.

In my journey as a Christian, I have come across students, teachers, accountants, doctors, lawyers, business people, engineers and people of all types of professions who are devoted Christians and have a desire to connect their faith to the work they do in their workplace. These Christians have a passion to influence the marketplace for the Kingdom of God and as a result, take their work very seriously and consider their workplaces as their primary mission field and a place where God has called them to be ministers of the Gospel. However, when I talk with some of these Christians, I discover many of them have felt isolated, and sometimes misunderstood by their fellow church members and even church leaders who tend to see them as "worldly" Christians because of the amount of time they dedicate to their work compared to the time they dedicate to other church activities. This is because many Christians and Christian leaders do not think ministry can be connected or done in the workplace (marketplace). The majority consider ministry to be limited to things like preaching, pastoring, and activities that take place in or around the church.

I have also come across Christians who are very pre-occupied with the work they do in church and consider any other activity outside their church activities as secular. Such Christians for instance will easily forgo any work they were doing in the workplace for church activities because they do not consider their work or workplace as a mission field for ministry. They consider work as just a temporal and necessary inconvenience they have to bear while focusing on the most important spiritual work which rotates around what they do in church. For them, to serve God and further the Kingdom, is to focus one's service to the things they do in the church; like attending services, ushering, cleaning, and doing evangelism. Besides, when such Christians decide to become full-time ministers, what they do is to totally give up their secular jobs and become full-time preachers or pastors. In summary, such Christians do not connect their faith to the work they do in their workplaces. These Christians have no passion to influence the marketplace for the Kingdom of God and as a result, do not take their work very seriously. They consider their workplaces as just a means through which they earn an income for their family and support the work of ministry done by the church through their pastors and other ordained ministers. I discovered most of such Christians are not very good employees in the workplace; because they do not approach their work with the focus and determination they need, to excel in the marketplace.

There is also a third category of Christians whom I want to call the nominal Christians. These are Christians who take their work very seriously and excel very greatly in what they do in the workplace but do not connect their faith to their work. These Christians do not take their faith in the workplace seriously. Though these Christians find some fulfilment in the work they do, they do not consider their faith to have any connection with their work in any way. So they have a kind of double life. When in church, they just flow with what is happening there but when they get to their workplaces, they operate by a different set of values which is not connected to their Christian faith in any way. These are a very dormant set of Christians who have great potential to influence their workplaces for the Kingdom of God. Unfortunately, they are not serving the interest of the Kingdom of God. They have put all their gifts and talents at the service of the world system and to the great disadvantage of the growth of the Kingdom of God and the church. Many of such people have no template on how to use their gifts and talents in the service of the Kingdom of God at the workplace.

It is for the sake of these *three* categories of Christians that I wrote this book.

The Lord is raising a great army of ministers in our time. These are not the traditional ministers like the ordained ministers leading churches but they are ordinary Christians in the marketplace. These categories of Christians are referred to as Marketplace Ministers and their type of ministry is commonly referred to as Marketplace Ministry.

To give you an idea, here are just a few quotes by some renowned men of God concerning Christians in the workplace (marketplace).

"I believe one of the next great moves of God is going to be through the believers in the workplace." Dr. Billy Graham.

"Societal transformation is high on God's agenda and the chief catalytic force to bring it about will be Christians ministering in the marketplace." C. Peter Wagner, author of The Church in the Workplace.

"God has begun an evangelism movement in the workplace that has the potential to transform our society as we know it." Franklin Graham.

The movement of marketplace ministry has been gaining momentum in many countries and churches around the world. For instance, in 2019, The Global Workplace Forum was organised by the Lausanne Movement (founded by Billy Graham in 1974). This gathering was the first of its kind in Lausanne's history, where the majority of the participants, 65% of the near 900 participants from 110 countries were Christians whose primary place of work is outside of churches or ministry organizations. They represented a landscape of the global workforce, from manual labourers to CEOs, entrepreneurs, and investors, blue-collar, white-collar, 'pink-collar', as well as 'no-collar' workers, those who work as home makers or caregivers in the often unseen workplace called home. Included were 200 virtual participants interacting with the programme and each other online. The goal was to better equip Christians for their ministry in the marketplace.

In this book, I outline the various facets of this ministry, providing definitions and explanations that can help the ordinary Christian as well the Christian leader to have a sound understanding of what marketplace ministry is all about. I have also put together some practical ideas on how a Christian can become an effective minister in the marketplace; which is a key to unleash the power of Heaven to transform society and draw in a massive harvest of souls into the Kingdom of God.

One of the main challenges with becoming an effective marketplace minister is the fact that the marketplace is a very different environment from what many Christians are familiar with within the walls of the church and the traditional Christian settings for ministry. There is a need for a shift in paradigm in how we do church and how we approach work/business as Christians.

In this book, I introduce some key mental shifts that need to occur to facilitate the equipping and the emergence of marketplace ministers in the body of Christ. I also put together practical steps which an ordinary Christian can begin to implement to transform their workplace into a place for ministry and become a marketplace minister. It is time for a marketplace shift in the body of Christ.

Chapter One

PARADIGM SHIFT
Five Paradigms that Must Change

"The "First" Reformation took the Word of God to the common man and woman; the "Second" Reformation is taking the work of God to the common man and woman. That time is now. The greatest potential ministry in the world today is the marketplace."

Tom Philips, VP of Training,
Billy Graham Evangelistic Association.

PARADIGM SHIFT
Five Paradigms that Must Change

WHEN I got born again, one of the first commitments or promises I made to God was to build churches. I was very passionate about the growth of the church and I am still very passionate about it today.

Immediately following this commitment came a very strong desire to be rich. I knew if I was to fulfil this promise to God, I needed to have a lot of money and so I decided I would put my energy and effort to become the richest Christian Entrepreneur in my time.

As I continued to nurse this passion, I began to search for Christian role models in business. I wanted someone to learn more from and who could mentor me in becoming a successful Christian Entrepreneur.

Unfortunately, that is where my frustration began. I realized in church when the preacher gives examples of successful people in business, he hardly ever mentions any renowned Christian.

In my mind, I kept thinking if there are no examples of successfully Christian Entrepreneurs in the church then, maybe church is not the place for me to learn how to become a successful business person. This was simply because the people the preacher kept quoting as examples, did not become rich by learning it in church and most were not churchgoers or committed Christians.

So, I figured out that I would probably have to learn that somewhere else, become the billionaire I want to become and then after that I can use the money to fulfil my promise to God.

Now pause for a moment and think about that. Does that make sense?

However, that was just the beginning of my frustration. Over the years, I also realized the *Christians* who ended up making the money, somehow had to disconnect with the *church* in order to do so.

Another observation was that most times it did not matter how such Christians made their money; if they can put such money in helping the church in its various programs and projects, they were generally accepted and welcomed. This only makes it worse!

To compound this problem, such people never dream of doing ministry. Because first of all ministry means preaching or doing something that is mostly restricted to the four walls of a church building or something closely related like going out on missionary trips. In fact, they know that for them to ever do ministry, they would have to give up their businesses or work to devote time to the ministry whenever such a call came.

Therefore, I concluded that being a pastor or minister was never going to be my thing. Besides, the only way I could ever fulfil my promise to God was to be a businessperson so I can make money and build the church or *support the ministry*.

Now, this was my thought pattern for several years as far as church and ministry were concerned. Many people probably still think the same way I did back then.

As I grew in my walk with God, there was always an uneasiness and a tension within me. I wanted to see Christians leading in different aspects of society and not just business. But, there was always this feeling of inadequateness; a feeling that something was missing.

It is during this period that God, by His grace, began opening my understanding to certain things about the gospel which led to a paradigm shift in my thinking. These paradigm shifts formed in me the foundation on how one can become a minister in the workplace and advance God's Kingdom effectively.

> There cannot be any successful advancement of the kingdom in the marketplace without a paradigm shift

In this chapter, I will introduce these five paradigm shifts and in the rest of the chapters, I will build on each of them to illustrate the shifts that must take place for Christians to become effective ministers in the workplace and advance the Kingdom of God in all spheres of influence.

One thing I must say is this; without these paradigm shifts, I believe there can be no effective ministry in the workplace and the church will not be able to advance the Kingdom of God effectively in the marketplace.

WHAT IS A PARADIGM SHIFT?

When I speak of a paradigm shift, it is important to understand what a paradigm is.

A Paradigm as defined by WordWeb Dictionary is *"The generally accepted perspective of a particular discipline at a given time."*

A Paradigm Shift, therefore, is *"a shift, change or adjustment in the generally accepted perspective of a particular discipline at a given time.*

In Luke 5:37-38 (*Passion Translation*), Jesus, responding to His critics and teaching His disciples says that no one puts new wine into old wineskins; because the new wine will burst the old wineskins and spill the wine. You must put new wine in a new wineskin. In other words, you cannot do a new thing with the old mindset, or the old pattern of how you use to do things. Trying to do so will only bring confusion and the result is that both the old thing and the new thing will suffer a calamity.

A paradigm is like a wineskin. To receive new wine also requires a new wineskin, a new paradigm.

There cannot be any successful advancement of the Kingdom in the marketplace without a paradigm shift.

In Luke 5:39, Jesus went further to say (paraphrased) *"But no one after drinking the old wine seems to want the fresh and new because they say the old ways are better and refuse to taste the new that I bring."*

One of the challenges in the church is that, sometimes, we try to implement new truths with old mindsets or old ways of doing things. The reason is that the old ways always *"taste better."* We think our old ways can contain the new thing God wants us to do. We think there is a way church has always been done; there is a way ministry has always been done; there is a way worship has always been done; and so any new thing must come through these old containers of our ways. We think we can receive the new thing God wants us to do while maintaining the old methods, the old ways which were passed down to us.

However, what I came to discover is that for the Kingdom of God to advance effectively in the marketplace in this age, there has to be a paradigm shift in the body of Christ. And by paradigm shift, I mean a radical and revolutionary way of thinking about everything we do as a church and as Christians. Without these paradigm shifts, we will try to put new wine in old wineskin and the result is that we won't see the benefits of the new wine God is pouring and the worse part of it is that, we will also lose the benefits of the old.

It is better to remain with the old ways (wineskin) and its old wine than to receive new wine in old wineskin. In other words, rather than trying to embark on Kingdom advancement in the marketplace (new wine) with old wineskin (old disciplines, methods of ministry), it is better to limit ministry to the old ways of just what happens in church on Sunday and continue in that light. Trying to blend the two only leads to problems. I learned this the hard way when I tried to implement the concept of marketplace ministry in a culture that did not embrace this shift. When I did this, I suffered greatly and the ministry did not prosper.

Five Paradigm Shifts that Must Happen

To effectively activate Christians in the workplace to advance the Kingdom of God, I have discovered these paradigm shifts, which must occur in the body of Christ.

- **Number 1: GOSPEL SHIFT**

A Shift in How We Present the Gospel

The very first paradigm shift that must occur is a shift in our understanding of the gospel.

For many people, the gospel is primarily about the Good News of Salvation: i.e. the Gospel of Salvation.

However, Jesus preached the Good News of the Kingdom of God. i.e. the Gospel of the Kingdom.

There is a difference between the Gospel of Salvation and the Gospel of the Kingdom. Have you ever considered the difference between the Kingdom of God and Salvation and what it is? When Jesus spoke about the Kingdom of God, what was He referring to?

Jesus spent an enormous amount of time talking about the Kingdom of God. In fact, the parables focus almost entirely on illustrating the different facets of the Kingdom of God. You will get a very different understanding of the world and things pertaining to the gospel, the church, ministry, and many other things when you truly grasp the scale and scope of the Kingdom of God.

- **Number 2: MINISTRY SHIFT**

A Shift in How We Do Ministry

When you hear the word "Ministry," what comes to your mind? Preaching? Church? Apostles? Prophets? Pastors? Evangelists? What about part-time and full-time ministry? What do these statements mean to you?

For many, the word "Ministry" or a "Minister" is an exclusive term reserved for Christians who have answered the call to serve God as Apostles, Prophets, Pastors or Evangelists within the body of Christ and in the church.

Paradigm Shift

What is your understanding of Ministry?

Is Ministry reserved for a special group of Christians within the body of Christ?

What does it mean to be called into the Ministry?

Is it proper for Christians to do Ministry on a part-time basis? Why? Why not? What does that mean actually?

The old paradigm of 'Ministry' need to shit if we must advance the Kingdomof God n the marketplace/workpace because in this age every believer is to be in full-time minisry.

The only difference between ministries is where they occur. Some ministries take place in the four walls of a church; some ministries take place outside the church.

The original meaning of the word ministry means "service." By this definition, wherever you offer a service, you are doing ministry. If you offer such a service as unto the Lord, then it is a valid ministry in the sight of God.

- **Number 3: WORSHIP SHIFT**

A Shift in How We Worship

Another important paradigm shift that must take place to effectively advance the Kingdom of God in the marketplace and produce effective marketplace ministers is our understanding of worship *and work*.

In the Hebrew language, there are two words for worship: *Shaw-khaw and Abad.*

Shaw-khaw means **to bow down, to prostrate.**

Abad means **to serve, to labour, and to work.**

Are you familiar with these two definitions of "worship"?

When Jesus said the time is coming when true believers will worship Him in spirit and in truth, what did He mean?

What did Jesus say about the *relevance* of *the place* of worship when it comes to worshipping God in spirit and in truth?

Does your understanding of what Jesus taught reflect the way most Christians worship God today?

When you combine the two definitions for worship, what new insights and understanding come to you when you think about worshipping God in spirit and truth?

These are the paradigm shifts that need to occur in the body of Christ for the advancement of the Kingdom of God in the marketplace.

- **Number 4: CULTURE SHIFT**

A Shift in How We Engage Culture

The fourth paradigm shift that must occur is our understanding and approach to the cultures of the world.

What is Culture? Culture can be defined as *"all the knowledge and values shared by a society"* or *"the attitudes and behaviour that are characteristics of a particular social group or organisation"*

In most Christian settings, we have a culture that identifies those who detach themselves from "worldly matters" as being more spiritual and dedicated to God than those who are active and involved in worldly matters. As a result, the church's main approach to the world's culture is to create a subculture, where we live in a bubble to the exclusion of the world, and demand that people in the world (including Christians) leave the world/culture and become part of our subculture in the church. This is a paradigm that also needs to change.

The church is called to go counterculture; engaging with the cultures of the world to transform them into a reflection of the Kingdom of God instead of running a separate and parallel culture to the cultures of the world.

Creating subcultures that alienates the rest of the world does not advance the Kingdom of God. It only tries to protect our interests and identities as Christians but does not do anything significant to reach out to the world and make disciples of all nations as Christ commanded us.

- **Number 5: CHURCH SHIFT**

A Shift in How We Do Church

The fifth paradigm shift is another very important shift which if not understood can greatly limit all the others.

Marketplace Shift

This for me is a very critical paradigm shift and probably the most important. Because without it, a lot of what I have been saying in the previous points will not be effective.

The "church" sometimes is the biggest threat to advancing the Kingdom. Now, let me explain before you shut me off. I believe that when the church is functioning as it should, it is the hope of the entire world! The question I have is, *"is the church functioning as it should?"*

This shift is even more critical for pastors and church leaders to get because if we do not get it, the members and particularly the marketplace minister/leaders emerging from within our congregations will experience great limitations.

We must shift our understanding and approach to church; we must shift from treating the church as a *cruise ship* and begin to look at church like a *battleship*. More on this in this book.

We must rediscover the true meaning of the "Ecclesia" which is the original word Christ used to describe the church. Ecclesia was never a religious term; it was and is a governmental term and speaks about the assembly like in a parliament or a national assembly. Jesus did not establish the church as another religious establishment to replace the Jewish synagogues.

POINTS TO PONDER

Now after that John was put in prison, Jesus came into Galilee, preaching the gospel of the Kingdom of God, and saying, the time is fulfilled, and the Kingdom of God is at hand: repent ye, and believe the gospel. (Mark 1:14-15).

◊ What do you know about the Kingdom of God?

If you do not know or understand what the "Kingdom" is, take some time to pray about it and study the following:

Jesus used parables to teach his listeners primarily about God and His Kingdom. Here are the Parables about the Kingdom:
- The Soils. (Matthew 13:3-8; Mark 4:4-8, Luke 8:5-8).
- The Weeds. (Matthew 13:24-30).
- The Mustard Seed. (Matthew 13:31-32; Mark 4:30-32; Luke 13:18-19).
- The Yeast (Matthew 13:33; Luke 13:20-21).
- The Treasure (Matthew 13:44).
- The Pearl (Matthew 13:45-46).
- The Fishing Net (Matthew 13:47-50).
- The Growing Wheat (Mark 4:26-29)

◊ Please take some time to review the headings of each of the five paradigms discussed in this chapter. To which of these five mindsets do you need to make a change in order to extend God's Kingdom in the marketplace?

REFLECTION QUESTIONS

- Do you consider yourself called into Ministry? If so, what is the ministry?
- What about your job, do you consider that a ministry? If you were to approach your work/job as a ministry unto to God, what would change about your work?
- What is worship to you?
- If your whole life was to be an expression of your worship to God, what would change about your life and why?
- What is your understanding of the world?
- How can you influence the world without being contaminated by the things of the world?
- Is it possible to change the cultures of the world without engaging with the world?
- What is 'church' to you?
- Consider the church as a community of people who live according to the teachings of Jesus in their everyday life.
- How will such a community look like?
- What activities will members of such a community be doing every day?
- How will their everyday activity compare to what they do on Sunday?

CHAPTER SUMMARY

The Five Paradigms that Must Change

- Paradigm Shift Number 1: Gospel Shift
- We must shift from Salvation only to a Kingdom Gospel.
- Paradigm Shift Number 2: Ministry Shift
- We must shift into a whole-life approach Ministry.
- Paradigm Shift Number 3: Worship Shift
- We must shift into a whole-life approach to Worship.
- Paradigm Shift Number 4: Culture Shift
- We must shift from an isolationist culture to an engaging culture with the World.
- Paradigm Shift Number 5: Church Shift
- We must shift from a Cruise mentality to Battle mentality of doing Church.

Chapter Two

GOSPEL SHIFT
A Shift in How We Present the Gospel

"Your Kingdom come, your will be done on earth as it is in Heaven"

(Matthew 6:10)

2 GOSPEL SHIFT
A Shift in How We Present the Gospel

I WANT you to imagine a conversation between Joshua and God. *"Now Joshua, I have called you to take the leadership from Moses and I want you now to take my people across the Jordan River into the Promised Land. However, once you cross the Jordan River I want you and all your people to sit down. Your mission is done."*

What do you think about this conversation? Can God tell Jo-shua that his mission is done just by crossing the Jordan River? Obviously not. We all know crossing Jordan River was never the goal, but a step into the ultimate goal of reaching the Promised Land.

> There are no two Gospels. There is just one; the Gospel that Jesus preached; which is the Gospel of the Kingdom of God

However, the majority of the church has actually been doing this. We have been preaching the Gospel of Salvation, but we have not taught people to apply the message of the Gospel to their everyday life and reach the Promised Land of God's purpose for the believer *which is the total dominion of God's Kingdom on the earth*. This is the difference between the Gospel of Salvation and the Gospel of the Kingdom. *Let me early on state here that there is really just one gospel; there are no two gospels. My point of presenting "two" gospels is for the sake of highlighting the difference in emphasis when we present the gospel in two different ways.*

In Luke 4:6-7, we read about the story of the temptations of Jesus. One of the most striking temptations the devil brought to Jesus was an offer of the kingdoms of this world with the only condition being that Jesus should worship the devil.

One key question to ask here is: Was Jesus really tempted? A Temptation is not really a temptation if is not about something you are interested in. This implies Jesus is actually interested in the kingdoms of the world. Another version does not just say kingdoms but also added, regions of the world.

For many people, Jesus is just interested in the souls of people: and not interested in the dominion of this world. However, the devil knows he who controls the kingdoms controls everything else, including the people in it.

> Jesus came to inaugurate a new government called the Kingdom of God

The very first paradigm shift in my thinking started when I was on a retreat, began reading my bible, and came across the scripture in Mathew 5:3 which says: *"Blessed are the poor in spirit; for theirs is the Kingdom of God."*

Throughout my life, I have always understood the gospel to be just about salvation until this point when God began opening my eyes to the full package of the Good News which Jesus preached *which is the Gospel of the Kingdom of God.*

It is from this point that I began understanding that Jesus spoke more about the Kingdom of God than about any other thing. To become an effective minister in the marketplace, you must have an understanding of the Kingdom of God.

Jesus talked about the Kingdom of God more than 70 times in the New Testament much more than He mentioned salvation. While salvation is part of bringing the Kingdom of God to earth, it includes much more. When Jesus came to earth, He came to penetrate the very kingdom of darkness with light. He came to bring healing to sickness, replace sadness with joy, and fill meaninglessness with purpose. He came to change things for the better for a world that had no hope outside of God.

Church Colson cites that *"Genuine Christianity is more than a relationship with Jesus, as expressed in personal piety, church attendance, Bible Study, and works of charity. It is more than discipleship, more than believing a system of doctrines about God. Genuine Christianity is a way of seeing and comprehending all reality. It is a worldview." (1)*

God wants you to bring the Kingdom of God into the territory He has given you so that His will can be done on earth as it is in Heaven. Your domain is your workplace, family, and community. When the Gospel of the Kingdom comes into a life and a community, it transforms everything in its path.

GOSPEL OF SALVATION VS GOSPEL OF THE KINGDOM

The simplest way to understand the distinction is the Gospel of Salvation deals only with salvation for your soul. The Gospel of the Kingdom deals with all things that the cross affected including salvation and reconciliation of all things, including the material world that was lost in the fall.

What do we mean by a kingdom? Dr. Myles Munroe describes a kingdom in these terms: "A kingdom is the sovereign rulership and governing influence of a king over his territory, influencing it with his will, his intent, and his purpose, manifesting a culture and society reflecting the king's nature, values and morals. A kingdom is the governing impact of a king's will over a territory or domain, his influence over a people, and a government led by a king." (2)

Jesus' desire was for God's Kingdom to be manifested on the earth. When He taught the disciples to pray, He petitioned His Heavenly Father by asking: *"Your kingdom come, your will be done on earth as it is in Heaven."* While we may never see God's kingdom completely manifested on earth as it is in Heaven, Jesus IS telling us that we should ask for it and expect it. Moses was led by God not to establish a religion but a nation of people who would love, serve, and honour God. In other words, God wanted His Kingdom expressed through their lives completely.

AN INCOMPLETE GOSPEL

The following comparison between attributes of the Gospel of the Kingdom and the Gospel of Salvation provides a better understanding of the two. When Jesus prayed the Lord's Prayer He prayed for the manifestation of what was happening in Heaven to happen on earth. *"Our Father in Heaven, hallowed be Your name, Your Kingdom come, Your will be done on earth as it is in heaven"* (Matt. 6:9-10). His emphasis was more than salvation.

Gospel of Salvation	Gospel of the Kingdom
Focus: Evangelism/salvation	Focus: Having Dominion
Eternal, heavenly focus	Material, social, earthly, secular.
Addresses only the soul	Addresses soul and body.
Rapture escape mentality	Possess the land mentality
Sacred vs Secular – dualism	Impact all aspects of society.
Goal: Transaction "Win the next soul"	Goal: Influence through servanthood, godly leadership, and active faith.

FACTS ABOUT THE KINGDOM OF GOD

In order to properly understand the mind shift that must take place in the understanding of the Kingdom, let me illustrate a few facts about the Kingdom of God:

The Kingdom of God is the realm where God's authority is established; and where God's authority is established, there is peace, righteousness and joy. All who come under the King's authority feel this peace, righteousness, and joy.

This implies that when the Kingdom of God comes into a house, peace comes into that house; when the Kingdom of God comes into a business, peace comes into that business.

The born again believer is an agent of the Kingdom of God and wherever he or she goes, the Kingdom of God goes with them. The believer has the power and authority to extend the power and influence of the Kingdom where he or she goes.

The Kingdom of God has the power to offer salvation to those who believe in and accept the authority of the King over their lives. This is the good news of salvation that the Kingdom of God brings.

By implication, it is very normal for people to experience the benefits of the Kingdom of God way before they become citizens of the Kingdom. In other words, become born again/saved. In practice, the more people experience the impact of the Kingdom, the more they are drawn to become citizens of the Kingdom. Jesus said, *"but if I cast out demons by the Spirit of God, surely the kingdom of God has come upon you"* (Matthew 12:28).

The Kingdom of God places emphasizes on discipleship which is what Jesus commanded His disciples to do. See Matthew 28:19. The Gospel of salvation focusses on "soul-winning" and the end result is, most times no real discipleship takes place; because once people get "saved," they do not see the need to change any further.

With a Kingdom mentality, people are discipled way before they get saved. With a Kingdom mentality, the focus is not to get people saved, but to get people to repent (change their way of thinking) to align with the principles of the Kingdom of God and ultimately to gain salvation in the process. So, people can be discipled long before they become born again. A nation, a community, a business, a family can be discipled long before all its citizens or members get saved.

WHAT DIFFERENCE DOES IT MAKE?

One key question that most people might be tempted to ask is what difference does it make? Is the gospel not about saving people? Whether it is called the gospel of salvation or the gospel of the Kingdom, is it not the same thing? Well, it is not.

One very important difference that comes with the understanding of the Kingdom of God is the role and purpose of the church. The Church's primary mission is to equip the saints so they can effectively carry out the work of extending God's Kingdom on earth. When we do not understand the Kingdom of God properly, the church will lose its focus and will not be equipping the saints effectively.

Jesus was the first person to utter the word, "church." Yet, He framed His ministry in terms of God's Kingdom breaking into our world, not into a church building. Just look at how Jesus introduced His ministry:

Jesus came into Galilee, proclaiming the gospel of God, and saying, *"The time is fulfilled, and the kingdom of God is at hand; repent and believe in the gospel."* (Mark 1:14-15 ESV).

Jesus framed His ministry in terms of the Kingdom of God, not the church. Do not get me wrong, I am not downing, dissing, or dismissing the church. The church is the Bride of Jesus (and we should love her Eph. 5:25); the church is the Body of Christ (and we should build it up Eph. 4:11-12). Yet, it was Jesus who framed the gospel as good news about a new reality (God's Kingdom) through the presence of a new King (Jesus).

THE KINGDOM AND THE CHURCH

Jesus spent more time teaching the disciples about the Kingdom of God than about the church.

We can deduce two things from this:

Firstly, maybe Jesus understood that His disciples would not have any difficulty understanding church, so He did not spend more time teaching them on it.

However, the disciples needed to properly understand the Kingdom of God because that was His original mission on earth and He needed them to understand it properly in order to spread it through the church, which He was going to establish.

In Mathew 16:18 and 19, when Jesus was establishing the church, He made some very important declarations about the church. Let's read them from the Message Bible:

> *"And now I am going to tell you who you really are. You are Peter, a rock. This is the rock on which I will put together my church, a church so expansive with energy that not even the gates of hell will be able to keep it out" "And that's not all. You will have complete and free access to God's kingdom, keys to open any and every door: no more barriers between heaven and earth, earth and heaven. A yes on earth is yes in heaven. A no earth is no in heaven."*
>
> (Matthew 16:18-19)

These scriptures clearly show firstly that the gates of hell are not coming against the church as most Christians tend to believe. The church is supposed to be an army with the primary mission of advancing and extending God's Kingdom on earth; ensuring every square inch of this earth is transformed to reflect Heaven. Without a proper understanding of the Kingdom and the purpose of the Gospel, the church will misuse its power and become irrelevant in the world.

There are several parables about the Kingdom of God and but none about the church.

Now, before you think I am diminishing the value of the church, let me just say this; I am not doing that. In fact, the more you understand the Kingdom of God, the more important the church becomes and more importantly the bigger the responsibilities of the church is.

> Salvation is the door to citizenship in the Kingdom of God here on earth, not just a ticket to Heaven

Putting the church before the Kingdom of God reduces the role and responsibilities of the church. This is because instead of the needs and goals of the Kingdom of God defining the role and responsibilities of the church, the opposite happens; the needs of the church instead reduces or diminishes the reach and extent of God's Kingdom.

One very negative consequence of this is the promotion of denominations instead of the Kingdom of God. That is Christians now equate the expansion of their church as the expansion of the Kingdom and it becomes a competition between churches fighting for members to grow their "own kingdoms or empires" instead of the Kingdom of God. This happens when we put the church before the Kingdom. We use the kingdom (powers of the Kingdom) to grow (gather) the church, instead of using the powers to expand the reach of the Kingdom by releasing the church (Christians) into the world.

> Heaven is for retirement. Earth is where we work to extend the Kingdom

The Kingdom of God grows as sons of the Kingdom influence the society with the values and culture of Heaven. A Godly society does mean a society where everybody is born again, it means a society where even those who are not born again (yet) are already experiencing the influence God's rule in their spheres of life, in education, economy, government, as God's kingdom agents take dominion and drive the affairs of society.

Another reason is that without this understanding, the scope of what we normally call ministry is reduced only to what happens within the church building. However, if we understand the Kingdom and view ministry from the perspective of the Kingdom of God (as Jesus did), then our scope of what ministry is, is much widened. We will now view Ministry in terms of how it serves the purpose of the Kingdom of God not just the purpose of the church.

An understanding of the Gospel of the Kingdom re-introduces you to the cultural mandate, which God originally gave Adam in the Garden of Eden in Genesis 1:26-28.

RELATIONSHIP BETWEEN THE CHURCH AND THE KINGDOM

The relationship between the Church and the Kingdom of God is often misunderstood. Christians often speak as if the Kingdom of God was just another name for the church. In fact, they are quite different from each other; and the Kingdom of God is much more important. The main thing that Jesus came to do was to establish the Kingdom of God. This is clear from the basic message that He proclaimed:

> *The time has come. The Kingdom of God is near. Repent and believe the good news*
>
> (Mark 1:15)

The gospels tell us that Jesus was constantly teaching about the Kingdom of God. The good news that He proclaimed was the gospel of the Kingdom or the Government of God. The twelve disciples were also sent out to proclaim the same gospel of the Kingdom (Luke 9:1-2). In contrast, the gospels only mention the word church twice.

The Kingdom of God is a much wider concept than the Church. The Kingdom includes every area of life that is under the rule and authority of God. If God rules a home, it is part of the Kingdom. Where a business is run on biblical principles, it is also part of the Kingdom. The Kingdom of God includes every human activity that is done according to His will.

God intends for His Kingdom to expand into every area of

life. This expansion takes place in two different ways. Individual people must be born into the Kingdom. Jesus said,

> *Unless a man is born of water and the Spirit, he cannot enter the Kingdom of God*
>
> (John 3:5)

As people are born again through repentance and faith in Jesus Christ, they become citizens of the Kingdom. God will deliver them from sickness and the power of the devil. Being born again is the only way that a person can enter the Kingdom of God.

The Kingdom also expands as Christians bring the different aspects of their lives under the will of God. As a Christian applies the principles of God's word to those activities where he has authority, they become part of the Kingdom of God. The Government of God expands as Christians extend the rule of God into the areas of life where they have authority.

This understanding should help us maintain a Kingdom mindset even as we do church. Because as we keep our minds focused on the message of the Kingdom of God, it helps prevent us from developing and adopting a "church/salvation only mindset" in our approach to the Kingdom of God.

A SALVATION-ONLY/CHURCH MIND-SET

A salvation-only mindset is one that makes Christians focus only on the church (i.e. ourselves and our personal salvation) and pay less attention to the rest of the world. It makes us to separate ourselves from the rest of the world (the unsaved) and to view life only in terms of those who are like us the church (i.e. *those saved and going to Heaven*) and those who are not like us – the world (i.e. those yet to be saved and are heading for hell.). It creates an *"us vs them"* mentality between Christians and the rest of the world.

Unfortunately, this mindset also has the negative consequence of creating an "us vs them" mentality even between Christians of different denominations. So Christians become more interested in differentiating themselves by their different expressions and denominations rather than using their uniqueness to work together for the greater purpose of extending God's Kingdom throughout the earth.

So, we end up losing sight of the bigger picture of extending the Kingdom of God, which requires the whole church going into the whole world with the whole (Kingdom) gospel; and not just a particular denomination or expression of Christianity.

The Salvation-only mindset creates a church-focussed mindset. And once we have a church-focussed culture, we begin to lose sight of the Kingdom mandate.

KINGDOM vs CHURCH/SALVATION ONLY MINDSET (3)

It's important to have an understanding of what it means to have a Kingdom mindset. In the table below, I contrast the Kingdom mindset and Salvation-only mindset (*which creates a church-focussed mindset*).

Kingdom Mindset	**Salvation-only Mindset**
Views being saved as the starting point of the gospel.	*Views being saved is the end-goal of the gospel.*
Views ruling creation (God's reign through us) as the end-goal of the gospel.	*Views escaping from creation (God rescuing us) as the end-goal of the gospel.*
Views bringing Heaven to Earth as the end-goal of the gospel.	*Views escaping Earth and going to Heaven as the end-goal of the gospel.*
Releases all saints as ministers in the marketplace.	*Merely trains people to serve in a pure church setting/environment.*
Views the church like an army in preparation to save the world from destruction by the (devil).	*Views the church like an ark for the safety of people escaping from the world/devil.*
Creates wealth to transform the community and contributes to nation-building.	*Motivates giving to build only our own church programs and projects.*
Is a holistic approach that integrates the gospel with politics, economics, and public policy.	*Insulates the gospel from politics and public policy.*

Views the Bible as a blueprint to structure every aspect of society.	*Views the Bible merely as a pietistic book that enables us to escape the world, enter heaven, and be spiritual.*
With a Kingdom mindset, churches embrace and love their surrounding unchurched/unsaved communities.	*With a salvation-only mindset, churches only embrace converted individuals within their communities.*
Trains people for all of life.	*Trains people only for church life.*
Nurtures leaders who are world system changers and "cultural creatives" who articulate the truth to society.	*Nurtures leaders who speak religious language relevant only to "saved/church" people.*
Speaks of the rule of God over the entire created order; over both the saved and unsaved.	*Speaks of the rule of God through pastors over the saved who belong in a church.*
With a Kingdom mindset, pastors release their people to their vocational callings in the marketplace.	*Controls people by marginalizing their marketplace callings and emphasizing only their church-based ministries.*
Applies a Spirit-empowered approach to the natural world.	*Involves a spirituality that separates from the natural world.*
Those with a Kingdom mindset are working toward a renaissance of Christendom.	*Those with a salvation-only mindset merely strive for a particular expression of Christianity; i.e. Denomination where they belong.*

Churches with a kingdom mindset equip 100% of the saints to fill up all things in every realm of life (Ephesians 4:10-12).	*Churches with a salvation-only mindset equip the 2-3% of the congregation called to be full-time pastors, ministers, and missionaries.*

For the Kingdom of God is not meat and drink: but righteousness, and peace, and joy in the Holy Ghost. For he that in these things served Christ is acceptable to God and approved of men (Romans 14:17-18).

But seek ye first the Kingdom of God, and his righteousness; and all these things shall be added unto you (Matthew 6:33).

Open your Bible and try to replace the word "Church" where it says "Kingdom of God" and read it and reflect on what you discover. Also, try the reverse. When you devote time to study Kingdom in detail, you will realise there is a lot more to know about the Gospel and the role of the church in spreading the gospel.

As believers, we are the church; when we gather together in a place, we are the "gathered" church; but when we go into the world of our communities and workplaces, we are the "scattered" church and it is in those places where we must demonstrate the reality of the Kingdom of God for a world that so desperately needs it.

The Kingdom of God is about righteousness, peace, and joy. How do you ensure righteousness, peace, and joy reigns in your home, in your community, in your workplace?

In the Beatitudes, Matthew 5:1-16, we have the longest recorded sermon of Jesus where He began describing the traits He was looking for in His followers. He said God blesses those who live out those traits. Each of the Beatitudes is an almost direct contradiction of society's typical way of life. In the last one, Jesus even recognizes that a serious effort to develop these traits is likely to result in opposition.

The best example of each trait is found in Jesus Himself. If our goal is to become like Him, applying the Beatitudes will challenge the way we live each day. This way of life is to be lived in every sphere of life as a demonstration of a superior Kingdom and way of life to the people around us.

REFLECTION QUESTIONS

Where or what is the Kingdom of God? What are the signs that the Kingdom of God is present in a place?

1. Does your everyday life reflect the priority of the Kingdom?
2. Can you list how God wants you to manifest the Kingdom of God in your family, school, or workplace?
3. If you were to ever suffer persecution, would it be for the sake of righteousness, peace, and joy? Would it be because you value the Kingdom above everything else?
4. As you read this chapter, what shifts have occurred in your mind? Do you agree with the distinction between the Gospel of salvation and the gospel of the Kingdom? If so why, if not why not?
5. How would you describe your primary mindset as you read this chapter, a Kingdom mindset or church/salvation only mindset?

CHAPTER SUMMARY

- Gospel of Salvation vs Gospel of the Kingdom
- There is a difference between the Gospel of Salvation and the Gospel of the Kingdom.
- The Kingdom is bigger than the Church.
- The Church is the primary agency for the Advancement of the Kingdom.
- The Kingdom Defines the Church's Scope of Work.

Chapter Three

MINISTRY SHIFT
A Shift in How We Do Ministry

"For rulers are not a terror to good works, but to the evil. Wilt thou then not be afraid of the power? do that which is good, and thou shalt have praise of the same:

For he is the minister of God to thee for good. But if thou do that which is evil, be afraid; for he beareth not the sword in vain: for he is the minister of God, a revenger to execute wrath upon him that doeth evil."

Romans 13:3-4

MINISTRY SHIFT
A Shift in How We Do Ministry

WHEN you read Romans 13:4, do you realise that Paul is referring to a government official as a minister of God? He does not just say he is a minister, but a minister of God! Now, that's something to pause for a moment and think about.

EXPANDING YOUR CONCEPT OF MINISTRY

Most of us think of ministry as the work done by pastors, missionaries, Christian conference speakers, or evangelists. We rarely think of work done by bankers, lawyers, engineers, or homemakers. We typically believe that those who get their paychecks from a church or other Christian organization are the ones who "*do*" ministry, while the rest of us are those to whom ministry is "*done.*"

This faulty way of thinking is a mindset that must change in the body of Christ. You must expand your vision of ministry so that you come to view all you do, regardless of your occupation, as what it can and ought to be - ministry that glorifies

God, advances God's Kingdom, and influences other people.

"The idea that service to God should have only to do with a church altar, singing, reading, sacrifice, and the like is without doubt but the worst trick of the devil. How could the devil have led us more effectively astray than by the narrow conception that the service of God takes place only in the church and by works done therein? ... The whole world could abound with services to the Lord ... not only in churches but also in the home, kitchen, workshop, and field." —Martin Luther.

The great reformer Martin Luther understood that ministry is more than just work done by pastors. We must start using the term ministry in a way that is much broader than the way the term is usually used.

DEFINITION OF MINISTRY (4)

A proper definition of ministry is *"the faithful service of God's people rendered unto God and others on His behalf to bring Him glory, build up His church, and reach out to His world."* Let's look at this definition in more detail.

THE FAITHFUL SERVICE OF GOD'S PEOPLE

The Greek word in the New Testament that is often translated as *"ministry"* is *"diakonia."* The basic meaning of this word is "service." It can refer to tasks as basic as waiting tables (see Acts 6:1), caring for the poor through monetary gifts (see 2 Corinthians 9:12), or proclaiming the gospel (see Acts 20:24). The term is not limited to the service of a select few appointed to particular offices within the church. In fact, the exact opposite is the case. Paul said that those who hold offices in the church are given gifts, to enable all of God's people to do ministry:

> *It was he who gave some to be apostles, some to be prophets, some to be evangelists, and some to be pastors and teachers, to prepare God's people for works of service [diakonia], so that the body of Christ may be built up.*
>
> (Ephesians 4:11-12)

The leaders of the church are not the only ones doing the work of service or ministry. The leaders are given to the church to prepare every member to do the ministry to render service to the Lord, to the church, and the world.

RENDERED UNTO GOD

In our fast-paced, high-tech world, we often fail to recognize that God is intricately involved in the details of our lives. Yet not only is God involved in our everyday routines, but He also wants us to be aware of and responsive to His presence:

> *So whether you eat or drink or whatever you do, do it all for the glory of God.*
>
> (1 Corinthians 10:31)

And whatever you do, whether in word or deed, do it all in the name of the Lord Jesus, giving thanks to God the Father through him.

(Colossians 3:17)

Whatever you do, work at it with all your heart, as working for the Lord, not for men, since you know that you will receive an inheritance from the Lord as a reward. It is the Lord Christ you are serving.

(Colossians 3:23-24)

Each of these exhortations from Paul's letters uses the phrase *"whatever you do."* This all-inclusive phrase points out that God wants to be prominent in our lives, in both the so-called *"significant"* things we do as well as the mundane things. We rarely think God is terribly concerned with our day-to-day activities in the boardroom, the classroom, or the bathroom, yet when our work is done *"for the glory of God"* (1 Corinthians 10:31), "in the name of the Lord Jesus" (Colossians 3:17), and *"as working for the Lord"* (Colossians 3:23), our work becomes an act of worship. Our work, however big or small, becomes ministry.

AND OTHERS ON HIS BEHALF

The ultimate example of ministry is Jesus Christ Himself. In Paul's letter to the Philippians, he told his readers that their attitude toward each other *"should be the same as that of Christ Jesus"* (Philippians 2:5). Paul went on to describe the kind of attitude he was referring to:

> *[Christ Jesus], being in very nature God, did not consider equa- lity with God something to be grasped, but made himself nothing, taking the very nature of a servant, being made in human likeness. And being found in appearance as a man, he humbled himself and became obedient to death even death on a cross!*
>
> (Philippians 2:6-8)

Jesus set aside the glory due Him and took on the form of a slave. His entire life on earth, and ultimately His death on the cross, was others-oriented. Paul's admonition to the Philippians and all of us as Christians is to imitate this others-orientation. This is particularly challenging in our culture, which is consumed with self.

For example, this cultural preoccupation often dominates our view of the way we make a living. We often think of our jobs in terms of the financial benefits they provide for us and our families. This isn't necessarily wrong, but we also ought to consider how our work can benefit others either customers who benefit from our goods or services or perhaps our co-workers, whose lives we can affect by serving them in times of need. If we are to imitate Jesus and thereby do the work of ministry to which we have all been called, we must learn to look at life with an others-orientation, in our workplaces, our homes, our churches, and every other arena.

TO BRING HIM GLORY

The Westminster Shorter Catechism begins, *"Man's chief end is to glorify God and to enjoy Him forever."* If this confession is true of all of humanity collectively and of each human being individually, then it should also be true of the pieces that make up the whole of our lives from the way we parent to the way we play, from the time we spend "on the clock" to the time we spend at the dinner table.

In the passage from 1 Corinthians quoted earlier, Paul said that activities as simple as eating and drinking can and should be done *"for the glory of God"* (10:31). God is glorified when we do anything with thankfulness, integrity, and our whole hearts. Thankfulness comes from a recognition that

> When we seek to glorify God in all we do, all we do becomes ministry

all we have and all we can accomplish comes from God. We fail to be thankful and to glorify God when we act and think as though we are self-sufficient rather than utterly dependent on Him.

Likewise, we live with integrity when our thoughts and actions are consistent with God's ethical intentions for His people. We compromise our integrity when our desires conflict with God's intentions.

Wholeheartedness means focusing on giving our best in all we do, not for the accolades we might receive but out of a desire to do what we do as unto Christ (see Colossians 3:23).

Now, just imagine if all Christians approach their whole life this way. If everything we do, be it eating, going to school, going to work, doing business, is all done with the primary purpose of glorifying God and not, self: there will be a revolution overnight — because there are millions of Christians in the marketplace today who do not approach their work this way.

As we go about our daily tasks with thankfulness, integrity, and wholeheartedness, God sees and is pleased. Others see and His reputation is enhanced He is glorified. When we seek to glorify God in all we do, all we do becomes ministry.

BUILD UP HIS CHURCH

Each of us has a special responsibility and has been uniquely gifted to minister to others. In his book *"Redeeming the Routines,"* theologian Robert Banks likens the coming together of Christians in a local church to the gathering of children for a birthday party. Everyone brings a gift; the only difference is that in the church, the gifts aren't for one person but everyone.

The New Testament makes it clear that all who have been born of the Spirit have been endowed with a spiritual gift (or perhaps multiple gifts). The main point of the New Testament discussion of spiritual gifts is that each of us, as individual members of the body, need the contribution of the entire body and conversely, the entire body needs the contribution of each member. Each of us in the body of Christ has needs, and each has something to contribute to others' needs.

As we come to see that as Christians we are all called to do ministry, we ought to reflect upon how God has designed and gifted us to build up His church.

AND REACH OUT TO HIS WORLD

In the book of Genesis, God gave a set of covenant promises to Abraham and his descendants. He promised that He would bless them and that through them He would bless "all peoples on earth" (Genesis 12:3; 28:14). Throughout Old Testament times, God wanted His people to be a missionary people who would visibly demonstrate to the pagan world around them that the Lord alone was the one true God. As God's beloved people, Israel had both a blessing and a purpose to make God known to the world. Psalm 67 captures these two themes of blessing and purpose: Too often the church focuses on the blessing and forgets the purpose of the blessing.

> We do "the Lord's work" when we do whatever we do for the glory of God and the good of others.

These same themes of blessing and purpose apply to Christians as well. We have been richly blessed through Christ and have been given a responsibility to spread the good news of

His Kingdom. This is not a job reserved for a select few; it is God's purpose for every Christian. Certainly, God has uniquely designed some to take the message of Christ to people in the far reaches of the world, but all of us have our own "mission fields" in our homes, neighbourhoods, places of employment, and the like. It is our responsibility to spread the gospel with our words and live out the gospel with our lives.

In his book *"The Other Six Days"*, R. Paul Stevens writes, *Throughout most of its history, the church has been composed of two categories of people, those who are ministers and those who are not. Ministry has been defined as what the pastor does, not in terms of being servants of God and God's purposes in the marketplace, the church, the home, the school or professional office. Going into "the Lord's work" means becoming a pastor or a missionary, not being co-workers with God in his creating, sustaining, redeeming and consummating work both in the church and in the world.*

My goal in this chapter and throughout this book is to present a different view of ministry, one more consistent with the teaching of Scripture. We do "the Lord's work" when we do whatever we do for the glory of God and the good of others. And that is how we advance God's Kingdom in the marketplace.

THE THREE MAIN CONTEXTS OF MINISTRY

As I said in the first chapter, with this new understanding of Ministry, there has to be a shift in how we do Ministry. I like to throw more light on this by showing us the different contexts where ministry takes place.

Throughout your day, you live in various contexts. Perhaps you begin your day talking with your husband or wife and children over breakfast. Then you head to the office, where you interact with co-workers and fulfil your tasks. Over lunch you meet an old friend from college. After work you stop by the school to pick up your son from school and have a conversation on the way home about his day. Maybe you see a friend at the grocery store or stop to greet your neighbour. Each day, you encounter a variety of contexts, or settings, in which you can have a ministry mind-set when interacting with others.

There are three broad categories of contexts in which you can minister: the world (*marketplace*), the church, the home.

The world or marketplace, as we will use the term, refers to the work we do and the interactions we have outside an explicitly Christian context and with people other than our families. This includes our jobs, our businesses, our neighbourhoods, our favourite restaurant, and our children's PTA meetings. The church represents not only things done at a church but also those things we do specifically with and for other believers (the term church in the New Testament is never used of a building but always of a gathering of believers). The home will refer to what we do with our families. These are all contexts in which we should fulfil our calling to minister.

Marketplace Shift

In each context, we have multiple roles. For example, in the world, you might be a manager, an electrician, a neighbour, and a football coach. In the church, you might be a deacon, an usher, and a financial supporter. In the home, you might be a wife, a mother, and a daughter. Reflecting on the roles you play in each context will help you understand that everything you do can be and should be an act of ministry.

The Home

The most important context of ministry is with one's own family members. There is no higher calling to other people than to one's own family. While your roles in your job and church are important, your role as a member of your family takes precedence. Ministry in a job or church should never make you neglect the calling to minister to your own family. Jesus demonstrated this principle when He provided for His mother by charging John with her care even while He hung on the cross (see John 19:25-27).

The Church

While many of us spend most of our waking hours doing our job, our workplace is not the only arena for ministry. Just as every believer should live a life of ministry in the world, every believer should also serve others in the church.

What does ministry in the church mean? It is ministry (service) performed explicitly as a representative of Christ with and for other Christians. It includes such things as leading a small group, being an usher, serving in a choir, doing evangelism on short-term mission trips, serving refreshments in a church meeting, serving on a clean-up team, and organizing other Christian meetings/gatherings.

Almost every church leader needs more labourers. There are more ideas for how Christians can serve each other and their communities than there are labourers to implement them. If you have been in a church where you are being ministered to but have not yet started ministering (serving) others in the church, now is the time to jump in and begin. The body of Christ needs each believer to serve in just the way God has gifted him or her—and to do so with excellence.

In chapter two, I spoke about the need to understand the Gospel of the Kingdom as opposed to the Gospel of Salvation. One of the effects of the gospel of salvation is that it has caused the body of Christ to view ministry only as what happens within the body of believers; limit any ministry to the world to just winning souls and getting people saved.

As a result, the majority of the Christians in the marketplace only equate ministry to when they are doing some form of work in the church. Any other service performed in the world, in meeting the social, economic and material needs of the society is not considered as ministry. However, when Christians begin to approach all of life as a service unto God, then even serving as a waiter in a restaurant can be a great means of demonstrating the Kingdom of God through a ministry backed by the power of the Holy Spirit.

The World (The Marketplace)

The third context of Ministry, which is the focus of this book, is Ministry to the World. Our roles in the world provide many ministry opportunities. In fact, the role in which most of us spend the majority of our waking hours is our occupation, our job. This implies our greatest time for ministry is not at home, not in church, but in the world.

In our job, we typically interact with both believers and unbelievers. In this role, we aren't financially compensated to be Christian witnesses (unless, for example, we work on a church staff). We are compensated to do a task or manage people. Even full-time parents, who don't have paying jobs, interact with shop attenders, school employees, and other children's families. The way we fulfil our responsibilities in our job is part of the ministry to which we have been called. In fact, it forms a greater part of it, because the greater part of our time is spent in the world.

> The Kingdom advances when we connect the spirit of revelation we learned in church with the spirit of wisdom that makes us shine in the marketplace

While this might not be the case for the pastors and church leaders; the average Christian spends more time in the world/marketplace than their pastor. Unfortunately, the greater part of the Christian's equipping is not designed to help them become effective ministers in the world/marketplace.

Consider the following Scripture:

> *For we are to God the aroma of Christ among those who are being saved and those who are perishing. To the one we are the smell of death; to the other, the fragrance of life. And who is equal to such a task? . . . Not that we are competent in ourselves to claim anything for ourselves, but our competence comes from God. He has made us competent as ministers of a new covenant—not of the letter but of the Spirit; for the letter kills, but the Spirit gives life.*
>
> (2 Corinthians 2:15-16; 3:5-6)

An attitude of service and a willingness to lay aside our interests for the interests of others should pervade our entire life. In this way, our jobs will be contexts for ministry. Ministry in that context involves both the way we interact with others and the way we accomplish our tasks.

> Ministry in the marketplace involves both the way we interact with others and the way we accomplish our tasks

We should do our work with a commitment to excellence. Adam and Eve were created to labour in

Eden. While it was an entirely pleasant labour before their fall, God intended them to do their work with excellence.

Likewise, God gives each of us labour to perform with excellence. Whether that involves changing diapers, writing computer software, ploughing a field, managing a marketing team, or framing a house, all of our responsibilities ought to be performed with our utmost effort and concentration.

How we accomplish tasks is not our only concern if we want to have an attitude of ministry at the workplace. The Christian worker should not have an "accomplish at all costs" attitude. The way we interact with others also counts. After all, our witness to those who don't share our beliefs and work ethic and our example to fellow believers who do is related to how we love more than to anything else. Love should be our chief characteristic (see 1 John 4:8). Our ministry at work involves both working as if we were working for the Lord and relating well with others.

> The Christian worker should not have an "accomplish at all costs" attitude.

Unfortunately, the body of Christ has not made much emphasis on this context of Ministry. The only context we are familiar with is the Church context of ministry.

However, for us to effectively minister to the world and advance God's Kingdom, we need to radically change our understanding and approach to the world.

We must place great emphasis on this context of Ministry. The purpose of this book is majorly on how we can advance the Kingdom of God in the world (marketplace); for that to happen we must refocus our ministries towards the world.

The consequences of the church's lack of focus in developing Christians to operate in this context of Ministry the workplace, has led to several Christians operating in the workplace and yet creating no impact for the Kingdom of God.

FOUR TYPES OF CHRISTIAN IN THE WORKPLACE (5)

Let me pose a question to you. I want you to think for a moment about the most significant Christians who have impacted the world for Christ in the last 100 years. Write them down. Name four or five off the top of your head. Don't read on until you do this for me. Then come back.

Now, look at the list. How many of those were full-time church ministry workers and how many were workplace Christians? My guess is your list is made up of mostly church ministry workers. People like Billy Graham, Benson Idahosa, Kathrin Kulman, Bill Bright, D.L. Moody or even Mother Theresa.

My point is, where are the men and women of faith impacting the world from the workplace? Why aren't we seeing them in the list? Absent are men like Jeremiah Lanphier (NY City revivals of 1857), RG LeTourneau (construction business who impacted many for Christ), William Wilberforce (England's statesman who demolished slavery) or Arthur Guinness, an entrepreneur who changed the society in Ireland and England at the turn of the century.

In his book "Anointed for Business" Ed Silvoso provides a thoughtful look at four types of Christians in the workplace. He cites the following four categories:
- The Christian who is simply trying to survive.
- The Christian who is living by Christian principles.
- The Christian who is living by the power of the Holy Spirit.
- The Christian who is transforming their workplace for Christ.

The Christian Who Is Simply Trying To Survive

The first category is best described as a person who has no purpose or zeal for their work or life. They have not seen the power or presence of God in their work life. Solomon describes this person:

So my heart began to despair over all my toilsome labour under the sun. For a man may do his work with wisdom, knowledge and skill, and then he must leave all he owns to someone who has not worked for it. This too is meaningless and a great misfortune. What does a man get for all the toil and anxious striving with which he labours under the sun? All his days his work is pain and grief; even at night, his mind does not rest. This too is meaningless.

(Ecclesiates 2:20-23)

This person most likely has a segmented life. Their faith life is segmented from their work life. They lack purpose and meaning and have little direction. They go to work to collect a paycheck and most likely their work is reduced to collecting a paycheck at the end of the month. They have never heard the voice of God in their life and would never consider praying during or for a workplace-related issue. They go to church, but they see the church as another place to do something for God. In the final analysis, this person is a defeated Christian simply trying to survive.

Unfortunately, the world is full of surviving Christians. They are waiting for the lifeboat of salvation to take them off this "evil planet." In fact, George Barna says that in America, 35-40% of the population claim to be born again. However, if you had forty per cent of the market share of your industry, how much influence would you have over that industry? Coca-Cola has a 40% market share in the soft drink industry. Do you think they carry a lot of clouts? You bet they do. But with 40% of the population of the U.S. born again, why is there still a lower degree of Christian influence in the society?

In a survey done by the Gallup organization in 1983, they measured the work habits of church-going people compared to non-churchgoing people. What they found was no significant difference between the morality and ethics of non-believers and Christians. Christians were as likely to steal company supplies, cheat on taxes and call in sick as the non-Christian.

Category 1 is a large segment of the Christian population.

The Christian Who Is Living By Christian Principles

> *But if you are led by the Spirit, you are not under law*
> *(Galatians 5:18)*

The second type of Christian in the workplace is the Christian who is living by Christian principles. We now live in a society that loves programs and systems to do things. We have 12 step programs and books that claim 7 steps to lose weight or 10 Ways to a Better Marriage as guaranteed formulas to achieve our goals. It's the motivational speaking industry at its best. For some, this type of programmed teaching is helpful. It gives them a track to run on. Christian authors use acrostics to help their audiences grasp key concepts.

In my book Dreams to Reality, I talk about the Humanistic Visionary who has mastered certain principles for success; which even the Bible teaches.

Let's face it: if the whole world lived on Christian principles we would definitely have a better world. However, this is still far short of the standard of God's Kingdom.

The Christian Who Is Living By the Power of the Holy Spirit

> *For as many as are led by the Spirit of God, these are sons of God. For you did not receive the spirit of bondage again to fear, but you received the Spirit of adoption by whom we cry out, "Abba, Father"*
>
> (Romans 8:14-16)

The key characteristic of a Level 3 Christian is best exemplified as one who has a heart toward God that hears the voice of God in every aspect of their life. They have moved past the Greek system and operate in the Hebraic model as the early church did. They understand that their life in Christ is a result of the love of God born in their hearts. They understand the grace of God and relate to God in loving obedience. Level 3 Christians know the importance of developing a heart toward God through prayer, the study of the Word of God, and obedience. They realise these are the three core ingredients to experiencing the power of God in their lives.

These are Christians who want to see the raw power of God manifested in the workplace in miracles, signs and wonders.

The Christian who is Transforming their Workplace for Christ

The Level 4 Christian is one who is transforming their workplace for Christ. Level 4 Christianity is a by-product or fruit of Level 3. You can only transform your workplace if you are moving in the power of the Holy Spirit. Jesus spoke of bringing the Kingdom of God to earth. Rarely did he speak of salvation as much as the Kingdom of God. Certainly, salvation was included in the Kingdom of God, but it included much more. Jesus mentioned the Kingdom of God 70 times in the New Testament (NKJV).

> *"This, then, is how you should pray: "'Our Father in heaven, hallowed be your name, your kingdom come, your will be done on earth as it is in heaven"*
>
> (Matthew 6:9-10)

When we talk of transformation, we are talking about bringing the Kingdom of God upon the workplace and society. The early disciples understood this.

> *"And these signs will accompany those who believe: In my name, they will drive out demons; they will speak in new tongues; they will pick up snakes with their hands; and when they drink deadly poison, it will not hurt them at all; they will place their hands on sick people, and they will get well"*
>
> (Mark 16:17-18)

> *"I will not venture to speak of anything except what Christ has accomplished through me in leading the Gentiles to obey God by what I have said and done - by the power of signs and miracles, through the power of the Spirit."*
>
> (Romans 15:18-19)

You see the supernatural was part of the normal Christian life.

Here are some examples of individuals who transformed or are transforming their workplaces for Christ.

JEREMIAH LANPHIER

Jeremiah Lanphier was a businessman in New York City who asked God to do something significant in his life in 1857. In a small darkened room, in the back of one of New York City's lesser churches, a man prayed alone. His request of God was simple but earth-shattering: "Lord, what wilt Thou have me to do?"

He was a man approaching midlife without a wife or family, but he had financial means. He made a decision to reject the "success syndrome" that drove the city's businessmen and bankers. God used this businessman to turn New York City's commercial empire on its head. He began a businessmen's prayer meeting on September 23, 1857. The meetings began slowly, but within a few months, 20 noonday meetings were convening daily throughout the city. The New York Tribune and the New York Herald issued articles of revival. It had become the city's biggest news. Now a full-fledged revival, it moved outside New York.

By spring of 1858, 2,000 met daily in Chicago's Metropolitan Theatre, and in Philadelphia, the meetings mushroomed into a four-month-long tent meeting. Meetings were held in Baltimore, Washington, Cincinnati, Chicago, New Orleans, and Mobile. Thousands met to pray because one man stepped out. Annus Mirabilis, the year of national revival, had begun. This was an extraordinary move of God through one man. It was unique because the movement was led by businessmen, a group long considered the least prone to any form of evangelical fervour, and it had started on Wall Street, the most unlikely of all places to begin.

R.G. LETOURNEAU

R.G. LeTourneau, a businessman from the United States, wrestled with the secular versus full-time Christian work idea. LeTourneau was a successful businessman in the early 1900s that recounts the turning point in his understanding of how God desires to use business for His glory. His pastor one day said to him, "You know, brother LeTourneau, God needs businessmen as well as preachers and missionaries." "Those were the words that guided my life ever since," said LeTourneau. "I repeat them in public at every opportunity because I have discovered that many men have the same mistaken idea I had of what it means to serve the Lord. My idea was if a man was going all out for God, he would have to be a preacher, or evangelist, or a missionary, or what we call a full-time Christian worker. I didn't realize that a layman could serve the Lord as well as a preacher. I left the parsonage in sort of a daze. If God needed businessmen, he could certainly find a lot better material than a dirt-mover with a lot of debts piled up in the garage business. But I said, 'All right, if that is what God wants me to be, I'll try to be His businessman.'" LeTourneau later became known for his generosity for giving 90% of his income to Christian causes.

GRAHAM POWER

Graham Power is the founder and Board Chairman of the Power Group of Companies, one of South Africa's leaders in the fields of civil engineering, development, and construction.

In 2001, Graham gathered 45,000 Christians in Cape Town, South Africa, to pray for the needs of the nation. Today this movement called Global Day of Prayer has become an annual global event involving millions of people from 220 different countries in which nearly every country in the world participates, praying for the needs of our world.

Graham also founded "Unashamedly Ethical" (www.unashamedlyethical.com) which is a campaign promoting ethics, values, and clean living through local communities all over the world. The campaign is built upon three pillars, around which local communities form: A challenge to people to make a public commitment to 'good values, ethics, and clean living'.

I was privileged to meet this amazing man of God in 2019 in South Africa when he came to teach a class of Christian leaders from over 30 countries and I was the delegate from Cameroon. That whole experience transformed my life.

HOTEL OWNER TRANSFORMS HIS WORKPLACE

Ed Silvoso, the author of Anointed for Business tells the story of a Philipino businessman who owned a hotel chain. God saved this man and began an amazing transformation that led to a major transformation in his large scale hotel. This man owned a 1,600 room hotel in three buildings. The hotel had become a haven for prostitution with the rooms being used as many as five times a day. The 2,000 employees had a primary clientele of prostitutes. There were more than 3,000 prostitutes. One of Silvoso's associates shared with the owner a formula for winning the lost. So, the owner of the hotel went out and hired 40 pastors and told them to follow these instructions.

Speak peace to the wolves. Bless those who curse you.

Eat and drink with the sinners. Become their friends.

Pray for them and their needs.

These were strict orders. They were not to share the gospel until these three requirements were met for two years. The net result of following these three rules was that all 2,000 employees got saved and the hotel was upgraded to an executive-level which removed the prostitution because the rates became too high. A prayer chapel was added with 24/7 prayer for anyone by dialling 7 on the telephone. Two years later 10,000 guests had received the Lord on this property.

Now, that is transformation!

Which Level Are You?

At what level would your spouse, colleagues or friends say you are? Start asking God to help you see how to transform your workplace today. If you are anywhere below a level 4 Christian at work, now is the time to purpose yourself to step into your full anointing – to transform your company, community, and country for the Kingdom of God.

CONCLUSION

The purpose of this chapter is to help you see your entire life your job, roles in the church, relationships within your family, and every other area of daily life as ministry. We have been called to love just as Christ loved. That doesn't necessarily mean we are to begin a travelling ministry like Jesus. Rather, we are to love others in all the contexts in which God has placed us. We are ministers of new life in Christ. Let us walk by the Spirit in an all-pervasive life of ministry. This is the shift that will enable us to advance the Kingdom in the marketplace.

REFLECTION QUESTIONS

There are three contexts of Ministry as we have seen in this chapter; home, church, and the world. Here are practical ways to institute a Ministry Shift.

1. Ministry to Family
- What is your primary ministry towards your family?
- How committed have you been in this ministry?
- What is God saying to you about this ministry?

2. Ministry to the Church
- What is your primary ministry towards the church? (the church is both local and universal; you need to first identify what is your ministry towards your local assembly).
- How committed have you been towards this ministry?
- What is God saying to you about this ministry?

3. Ministry to the World/Marketplace
- What is your primary ministry towards the world? (This can refer to your workplace, business, school, etc.)
- How committed have you been towards this ministry?
- What is God saying to you about this ministry?

For all three contexts of Ministry, you should also ask yourself the question: Have I been operating in the full power of the Holy Spirit in each of these Ministry contexts?

CHAPTER SUMMARY

1. Definition of Ministry.
- The Faithful Service Of God's People
- Rendered Unto God
- And Others On His Behalf
- To Bring Him Glory,
- .Build Up His Church,
- And Reach Out To His World.

2. The Three Contexts of Ministry.
- The Home
- The Church
- The World/Marketplace

3. Four Categories of Christians in the Workplace.
- Surviving Christian
- Good Testimony Christian
- Power Christian
- Transformation Christian

Chapter Four

WORSHIP SHIFT
A Shift in How We Worship

"Put your heart and soul into every activity you do, as though you are doing it for the Lord himself and not merely for others"

(Colossians 3:23)

WORSHIP SHIFT
A Shift in How We Worship

MOST Christians think of worship as something they do inside the church building. And most also believe that to get really committed to Jesus means getting busy at the church: serving at the church, attending group meetings; going on a mission trip, etc. *We have already seen in the previous chapter that church is only one context of ministry.*

And there is also this kind of thinking that for Christians, our jobs (your work or secular jobs) are just necessities that must be endured to put bread on the table.

If God has any interest in your jobs, it's just that you don't cheat and that you faithfully pay tithe of your salary. And so many people approach work as just a means to get money to fund the work of ministry.

Is that what it means to serve God in your work?

Well, believe it or not, the Bible actually has a lot to say about our work. We need to change our mindset about work. In Genesis 2, at the first mention of work in the Bible, the Hebrew word God uses for it is *"abad,"* which shares the same root word as worship.

Adam worshipped God in the Garden not just by reading the Bible and praying and staying away from a few bad apples; he also worshipped God by doing the work God put him in the garden to do. Our worship is to be a daily expression of adoration to who God is and our devotion to His service.

There are two words for worship in the Bible. I will like us to study these two words closely:

Shaw-khaw: *To bow down, to prostrate.*

The first word used for worship in scripture is shaw-khaw and it means in very clear terms to bow down or prostrate. In other words, one way to worship God is by simply bowing down to Him or prostrating before Him. Obviously, this must come from a heart that genuinely loves God for it to be meaningful. We must develop the habit of bowing before Father regularly, as a sign of our worship/reverence to Him.

> Our Worship is to be a daily expression of adoration to His Person and devotion to His service

Abad: *To serve, to labour, to work.*

The second word used for worship in scripture is abad and it means to *serve, to labour, and to work*. It also means to work for another, serve another by labour. It can also mean to make oneself a servant. In other words, another way to worship God is to serve, to labour or work for Him. This brings a very important point to consider and a question to ask. How does one serve, labour or work for God?

The only way we serve God is by serving others.

This has enormous implications for us as Christians. There are two primary ways in which God expects us to worship Him. The first is bowing to Him, the second is by working for Him, and the only way we work for God is by working for others. The only way we serve God is by serving others.

Surely it cannot be coincidental that the majority of the parables that Jesus told had a workplace context. And of the forty miracles recorded in the book of Acts, thirty-nine of them occurred outside of a church setting. It is apparent that the God of the Bible is as concerned with displaying His power outside the walls of the church as He is within it.

8 TENETS OF WORK AS WORSHIP

With these two different meanings of worship, how then can we see work as worship? We need to understand some fundamental truths about work. Here are eight truths about work.

Work Is Good

In the beginning, God created everything including work. And as with all things He created, work was good. Free from toil and adversity, humans worked in the garden as an expression of worship to God. In its original created form, work was one of the ways humans engaged in relationship with God. As those made in the image of the working God, humans also worked—and it was good. Genesis 1:28; 2:15.

Sin Corrupted Work

The pure goodness of work didn't last forever. In one disobedient act, humans severed their relationship with God. Sin caused a ripple of destruction throughout all creation. As a result, work was also broken, corrupt, and cursed because of the Fall. Instead of worshipping God through work, we tend to worship the hollow god of work. Work can cause personal stress, relational tension, and global problems. Work was in desperate need of redemption. Genesis 3:17–19, 23.

Jesus Makes It Possible For Work To Be Redeemed

God wanted to make things right again, but sin couldn't go unpunished. Compelled by His love and mercy, He sent His Son, Jesus, to pay the price for sin. Jesus paved the way to redeem us and redeem work through us. He died and rose again not just to save sinners, but also to restore all of life, including work. By grace through faith, Jesus renews us and our approach to work. Work is no longer broken with no hope for repair. Work no longer rules over our lives. With God's favour upon us, we don't work to earn His approval. We work motivated by the love of our Saviour. In Christ, we are free to work for God's glory. Ephesians 1:7–10; 2:1–10; 2 Corinthians 5:21.

God Gave Us A Mission

When Jesus left the earth, He commissioned His followers to the mission of God to extend His Kingdom and make healthy disciples who grow in Christlikeness and love God's Word. God gifted us with the Holy Spirit who now lives in us, empowering us to fulfil God's mission until Jesus returns one day to restore all things. With this new perspective of life, we are on mission for God wherever we go even at work. Work has a role in the Kingdom of God because work is an avenue for fulfilling God's mission. In fact, we have more opportunity to minister to people and to spread the Kingdom of God through our work than in any other place.

With a newfound purpose, we chase God's mission with perseverance in the boardroom, the construction site, or the classroom. Because of Christ and His mission, we have purpose in all we do, especially our work. Matthew 28:18–20; Acts 1:8; Hebrews 12:1–3.

We Carry Christ Into Our Work

Compelled by God's mission, we carry Christ with us wherever we go. Following Jesus isn't limited to Sunday morning-spirituality and work aren't separated. All of life qualifies as spiritual as we carry the truth of Christ into the workplace. We are Jesus's ambassadors at work in the conference room, in the market, or at the lunch table. We represent Him as lights in the darkness of the marketplace. Everything we do at work should be done in the name of Jesus, motivated out of adoration for Jesus, and presented with the love of Jesus. Colossians 3:17, 23–24; 2 Corinthians 5:20.

God Grows Us Through Our Work

When we enter into a relationship with God through Jesus, God grows us into the image of His Son. The Spirit of God works in us as we work. He uses our relationships, successes, failures, and experiences at work as a significant tool in our spiritual formation. He teaches us to have the mind of Christ at work, to treat people as Jesus did, 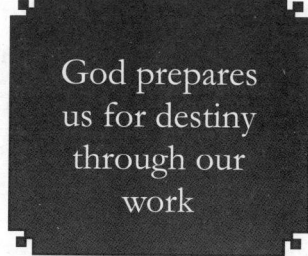 and to bear the fruit of the Spirit. We make mistakes, learn, and grow in our jobs under the guidance of the Holy Spirit. Through work, God shapes how we view Him, the world, and ourselves. We become mature followers of Jesus as we pursue God at work. Ephesians 4:14-16; Philippians 1:3-6.

God prepares us for destiny through our work

I can tell you that from my personal experience that God has moulded me in so many ways through my job. Many Christians who have character problems will find that working on a job will reveal that character faster than just sitting idle in church. Many times I recommend people to take a job because I know how much God can work on their character through the job. In fact, most people who believe they have a vision to start their own business or organisation, I always tell them until you take up an actual job working for somebody else, you will never be truly equipped to run your venture. It is a Biblical principle that can only be fulfilled by taking up a job. Joseph worked for Potiphar before he was made Prime Minister, Jacob worked for Laban before God gave him his own. God prepares us for destiny through our work.

God Can Do More With Our Work Than We Can Imagine

God does more through us at work than we can ever imagine. He designed work for the good of the world not just ourselves. God sees our small acts of obedience at work and those actions have a profound impact in His kingdom. Our work impacts our co-workers, clients, and managers. It also provides jobs, fuels the economy, and allows culture to flourish. In some ways, we may never know the profound impact of our work, but we can trust that God uses work to influence people around the world. Matthew 13:31–33; 25:29; Mark 10:45.

Work is Worship

Our work goes beyond being a mission field, a place of growth, and an avenue for impact. Work is also worship. Everything we do work included can glorify God and honour His name. God gives our work purpose. He uses it to mature us. And He uses our work to reach people and communities. When we work, we taste the goodness God intended for work in the beginning. 1 Corinthians 10:31; Matthew 22:37–39.

FIVE WAYS YOU WORSHIP GOD WHILE YOU WORK. (6)

Based on these eight (8) tenets of Work as Worship, I want to suggest to you five ways you worship God while you work.

1. 'Worshipful' Work Fulfils God's Purposes in Creation (Genesis 2:15).

God placed Adam in the Garden of Eden, with the assignment *"to work the ground and keep it."* This was before the curse. So work was not a punishment inflicted on Adam for his sin. It was a part of God's original design.

The word for work literally means *"to prepare"* or *"to develop."*

God made Adam be a gardener. A gardener is not a park ranger who just guards the garden. God put Adam there to develop it. He was to take the raw materials of the earth and develop them for the glory of God and the benefit of humans. He made man in His image, and as God was a creator, He put Adam in the garden to be a co-creator.

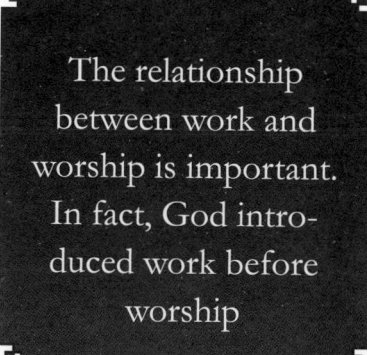

The relationship between work and worship is important. In fact, God introduced work before worship

Do you remember the word God used for His creation? "Good." Good is good, but good is not perfect.

Marketplace Shift

Perfect means cannot be improved upon. God created the world raw, in a "good" state, so that we could develop it and cultivate it for His glory and others' good. We take the raw materials of the earth and develop them for God's glory and the benefit of humans.

Contractors take the raw materials of sand and cement and use them to create buildings. Artists take the raw materials of colour or music and arrange them into art. Lawyers take principles of justice and codify them into laws that benefit society. As we do this, in a way, God is Himself at work creating through us.

The Reformer Martin Luther took Psalm 147:13, which says,

"For God strengthens the bars of your gates; he blesses your children within you. He makes peace in your borders; he fills you with the finest of the wheat." And he asked:

How exactly does God do those things?

How does He strengthen the bars of the city? By city planners and architects; by politicians who pass good laws to protect the city.

How does He bless our children within our midst? Through the work of teachers and paediatricians.

How does He make peace in our borders? Through good lawyers and policeman.

How does He fill us with the finest of wheat? By using farmers and factory workers and restaurant owners.

Our professions, Luther said, are like the "masks" God wears in caring for the world.

He said this: "When we pray the Lord's Prayer we ask God to 'give us this day our daily bread.' And he does give us our daily bread. He does it by means of the farmer who planted and harvested the grain, the baker who made the flour into bread, the person who prepared our meal." All these are in play when God answers our prayer for daily bread.

There are two Old Testament figures in Exodus 31, Bezalel and Oholiab, whom Moses says were filled with the Spirit.

How did they express that? By being expert craftsmen. Their expression of being filled with the Spirit was doing excellent work.

For many people, work is not just about money, it's about co-creating with God; taking the raw materials God gave humanity and producing something beautiful or perfect out of it. We are co-labourers with God.

God gave the good raw material and man is to get to work transforming it into anything he wants for the benefit of society. And God is pleased when we do that.

2. 'Worshipful' Work Pursues the Highest Standards of Excellence

If our work is done "unto God," it should be done according to the highest standards of excellence: as an offering to God!

Paul says, *"Whatever you do, work heartily, as for the Lord and not for men, knowing that from the Lord you will receive the inheritance as your reward. You are serving the Lord Christ.* (Colossians 3:23–24)

You have a higher boss than your employer; you work for a greater reward than your salary. In everything we do, Paul says, we do it unto God, which means we do it as a statement about the worthiness of our God.

C.S. Lewis once noted how valleys undiscovered by human eyes are still filled with beautiful flowers. For whom did God create that beauty, if no human eyes would ever see it? Lewis answered that God does some things only for His pleasure. He sees even when no one else does.

Christians make beautiful things for God often even when no one else notices.

Someone says, *"Well, my boss is terrible. He doesn't reward me properly; he doesn't ever give me the recognition."*

But you're not really doing it for him. You're doing it for God.

Interestingly, many of the people to whom Paul is writing had the worst possible boss situation. Paul says, "Slaves, obey your masters."

You might say today that your boss totally owns you. For the believers in the days of Paul, it was literal. And even there, in the worst and least rewarding circumstance, they were to do their work unto God as a statement of His worthiness.

Paul says that this is one of the things that should set Christians apart: they do their work for the glory of God. Whether we eat or drink or mop floors or write contracts, we must do all to the glory of God.

In everything we do we say, "The way I do this is a statement about your worthiness God! I do it for you!"

3. 'Worshipful' Work Reflects the Highest Standards of Ethics

Lack of integrity is nothing new in the workplace, but work that worships God will conform to the highest standards of ethics because it seeks to demonstrate the justice and integrity of God.

Business ethics really matter to Christians because our work is done unto God and our ethical practices reflect on God.

God says in Proverbs 11:1, *"A false balance is an abomination to the LORD, but a just weight is his delight."*

A "false balance" means: a false business expense report,

calling in sick when you are not, appropriating office supplies for personal use, unreported income…All these are an "abomination" to Him.

To worship God in your work means having standards higher than even the world! It means going beyond even the world's standards.

I can't tell you how many Christians I've heard say that they don't like to do business with "other Christians." These are not people in the world, but Christians talking about themselves.

How on earth are we to be the light of the world if we cannot trust our fellow Christians to have integrity in the workplace? It is an abomination to come and bow down to God in worship on Sunday and then on Monday you are lying to your boss in the office!

Psalm 15:1–3 (The Message): "God, who gets invited to dinner at your place? How do we get on your guest list?

God says: 'Walk straight, act right, tell the truth. Don't hurt your friend, don't blame your neighbour for things you did… Keep your word even when it costs you, make an honest living, and never take a bribe."

4. 'Worshipful' Work Makes Blessing Others Its Bottom Line

To follow Jesus means that you think about your life the way He thought about His: as an offering to serve others (2 Cor. 8:9). That's what you do when you follow Jesus. You begin to leverage your place of strength to bless and serve others like Jesus leveraged His for us (Luke14:12–14).

What does that look like?
- It may just be your attitude:
- The joy of service.
- Forgiving somebody.

There is a story about a young college graduate who landed a job on Madison Avenue in one of the advertising world's most prestigious firms. Shortly after she got there, she made a mistake that cost the company nearly $25,000. Madison Avenue is not a world defined by grace, and she expected to be fired by the end of the day. Her boss, however, went before his board of directors and convinced them to allow the blame for her mistake to fall on him instead. When this young woman heard what her boss had done, she came to him in tears. She asked him why, in that cutthroat atmosphere, he would choose to cut his own throat for her. He answered by sharing how Jesus had done a very similar thing for him, stepping in the way of the wrath that he deserved. Because of the great grace that Jesus had shown him, he wanted to display similar mercy to others when he could.

For you who own businesses: It means you think about more than merely personal profit in your bottom line.

> Those who experience the gospel become like it.

You'll start to ask questions like, "I know we can make a profit from this, but is it genuinely helpful to people?" Or, how can I use this business not just to enrich myself, but to bless others?

Now, I'm not trying to say there is any dichotomy between those two. People often think "profit" and "business" is bad. A good, profitable business is one of the greatest benefits to the poor. Good business makes the water in the harbour rise so all the boats will rise not ZERO SUM.

But it means that you think not just about personal profits in your business, but the blessing of everyone involved.

Medical professionals may see that some practice is legal and makes money but doesn't add benefit to people's lives.

Certain kinds of development may be good for few, but harmful for the community.

And it will probably mean you give away a lot of the personal profits you make from the business. Because that's what Jesus did for you. Those who experience the gospel become like it.

HOW TO BE AN EFFECTIVE WITNESS IN THE WORKPLACE

Many people wonder how to be an effective witness for Jesus in the workplace. Just doing these 4 things will set you off as a completely different community.

Peter said, "In your hearts honour Christ the Lord as holy, always being prepared to make a defence to anyone who asks you for a reason for the hope that is in you." (1 Pet.3:15 ESV).

> Most of the countries in the world in most need of a gospel presence are also those in the greatest need of business development

Peter's context is like ours. We were to live in such a way that people had to ask about our motives.

Honouring Christ first in the business place, means doing business according to these 4 things fulfilling the creation; with excellence, integrity, and to bless others.

Doing it in a way that will make others ask: why. Do you work so hard, with such excellence, integrity, and grace that people sense the reality of hope and an invisible Kingdom that they just have to ask about? If you do, then your work has become a form of worship to God, as it is ministering the reality of God's goodness to the people around you.

5. 'Worshipful' Work Seeks To Advance Jesus' Mission Where It Can

Work done by disciples of Jesus should be done with a view toward the Great Commission because that is our marching orders!

> Do what you do well for the glory of God; do it somewhere strategic for the mission of God

Billy Graham says the next Great Awakening will likely take place in the workplace.

The next wave of missions will be on the wings of business.

Most of the places in the world in need of a gospel presence are also those in the greatest need of business development.

If you lay a map of world poverty out and overlay it with one showing the places in the world that are the most un-evangelized, you'll see an incredible amount of overlap.

That means Christian business people and entrepreneurs have an incredible amount of opportunity!

Maybe God made you good at that skill so you could take it to places where He is not known.

What if God made you good at that skill to open up a whole nation or region to the gospel and give you an inheritance in an eternal kingdom?

Not every Christian, of course, will be led to perform their business in an unreached people group. But I want to challenge you to ask the question.

> "Do you see a man skilful in his work? He will stand before kings; he will not stand before obscure men."
>
> (Proverbs 22:29)

Do your work well and then stand before the lost kings of the earth so that the nations will worship!

WORSHIP GOD, NOT YOUR WORK

When Adam and Eve fell, our relationship to work changed. Instead of being something we pursued to glorify God and serve others, work became one of our primary sources of identity and idolatry.

We define our worth by the status of our job or maybe even by the fact that we don't have to work.

We depend on the security of our job to take care of us in the future. You can see this change in relationship to work in the descendants of Adam and Eve (Genesis 4). Two lines descended from Adam and Eve.

The Descendants of Cain

Cain who killed Abel and was driven out by God into the wilderness his descendants developed agriculture, music and metal great workers, like they were supposed to be, but the thing to notice is that they were defined by their jobs.

This culminated in Genesis 11, at the tower of Babel, in which they built this magnificent tower; a great achievement, but it was to make a great name for themselves.

What God gave to us as a means of saying, "Look at God and worship him," has now become a means of saying "Look at me (my work), and be impressed."

The Descendants of Abel

In contrast to the descendants of Cain, the descendants of Seth (godly line) were not defined by work, but were defined instead as *"those who began to call upon the name of the Lord."* (Gen. 4:25).

The point is not, of course, that they didn't work, or worked less. The point is that worshippers of God are not defined by their work. It does not matter the type of work or where the work takes place. It does not matter whether the work takes place in the church, in the office or at home. Instead, true worshippers are defined by the name of the Lord whom they worship.

Because of the fall, many of us worship our work, making it our identity. We also make it our security.

Work is a terrible god; God is a great God. He's the One you can depend on. He's the One who has taken care of your ultimate problem is not lack of money or status, but death. He gave you the life you are living. Your work or job did not!

And this applies to all forms of work, even working in a church or "ministry" setting can be a problem. There are pastors whose identity and security is tied to the "ministry" this is not the plan of God for any work we do.

Work matters to God; God matters to work

Robert Briner, Roaring Lambs:

"There should be no less support or attention for an earnest Christian young person who has been accepted to the Juilliard School of Music than for one going off to a theological seminary. The church needs writers, performers, artists, speakers, politicians, businessmen, businesswomen, and workers in every craft and trade. In God's eyes, there is no hierarchy, there certainly should not be in ours."

Artists, Musicians, Athletics, Creatives, Advertising, Marketing, Film, Television, Web or Print Design (they all stand alone no one understands them).

Entrepreneurs, Business Owners.

Healthcare, Pharmaceutical, Biotech, Medical, or in some facet of the field of science.

Marketplace Shift

Government, regional, local, including the military; Law, Finance, Accounting, Tax; Social Services or the Non-profit sector.

Real Estate, Construction, Architecture, Transportation or in trades such as plumbers, electricians, painters, mechanics or carpenters.

Service industry, such as Retail, Food Service, Hair Stylist, Chefs.

Business, Technology, Coaching, Consulting, Professional Services, Education, Engineering, Manufacturing.

All the above sectors are different avenues in which more than 90% of Christians go to every day. These are opportunities to glorify God and fulfil the mission of extending God's Kingdom if we learn to worship God through our work in these domains.

Work is worship when you fulfil God's purpose for creation: you prepare and develop the earth for the benefit of humans and the glory of God. You are God's mask, and he is working through you.

REFLECTION QUESTIONS

As we have seen in this chapter, worship has two roots which include service to God and homage to God.

Here are practical ways to institute a Worship/Work Shift.

Do you consider your current job/work as a form of worship to God? If so, why? If not, why? Write down your reasons; take them to God in prayer, share with your pastor and get feedback on what you have written.

1. Would your friends/colleagues say you approach your work/job as a service unto God? Would you say you worship God through your work or do you worship the god of work?

2. Have you ever offered/dedicated your job, work or business to God to be used solely for His purpose? If not, would you consider doing so now? And are you willing to make the necessary changes God might ask you to do to ensure your worship is acceptable to Him through your work?

CHAPTER SUMMARY

1. Work is a form of Worship.

2. Eight Tenets of Work as Worship.
    i. Work is good.
    ii. Sin corrupted work.
    iii. Jesus makes it possible for work to be redeemed.
    iv. God gave us a mission.
    v. We carry Christ into our work.
    vi. God grows us through our work.
    vii. God can do more with our work than we can imagine.
    viii. Work is worship.

3. Five Ways We Worship God through Work.
    i. 'Worshipful' work fulfils god's purposes in creation.
    ii. 'Worshipful' work pursues the highest standards of excellence.
    iii. 'Worshipful' work reflects the highest standards of ethics.
    iv. 'Worshipful' work makes blessing others its bottom line.
    v. 'Worshipful' work seeks to advance Jesus' mission where it can.

4. Worship God, Not Your Work.

Chapter Five

CULTURE SHIFT
A Shift in How We Engage Culture

"All these kingdoms, all their glory, I'll give to you. They're mine to give because this whole world has been handed over to me."

(Luke 4:6)

CULTURE SHIFT
A Shift in How We Engage Culture

IN Mathew 4:8-10 and Luke 4:5-6, we read about the temptations of Jesus and in this particular instance, the devil showed Jesus all the kingdoms of the world and their glory and offered it to Jesus if only He would worship him.

With a renewed understanding of the Kingdom of God, I developed a much bigger outlook on the world as a Christian. Now, I realize I have a world to bring under subjection to the King of kings, Jesus Christ. Salvation was just the doorway, just the beginning; the ultimate goal was to bring the kingdoms of this world under subjection to the Kingdom of God; the kingdoms that the devil so proudly claims are his to give to whomever he chooses.

When you have an understanding of the Kingdom of God, the temptations of Jesus in the wilderness begins to make a lot more sense.

One of the tricks of the enemy is to deceive us Christians to become too "church focused" and forget about taking over the kingdoms of this world or for those whose eyes are open to pursuing the kingdom, he attempts to give them access to the kingdoms through compromise as he tried to do with Jesus.

Either way, the enemy has his eyes focused on the kingdoms of this world while the Christians continue to play "church."

When we understand the focus of Jesus (the Kingdom of God), then the church will be awakened to its true potential and begin to take on its true responsibilities.

We build the church (God's people) so that it is equipped for the work of expanding God's Kingdom in the world. However, without this understanding, it is easier to equate church growth to Kingdom expansion. That the church is growing (in number) does not mean the Kingdom of God is expanding. The Kingdom of God only grows when the church imparts its values to the kingdoms of this world. Influence in the world is not a function of numbers only; it is a function of who occupies the key positions of influence in society; who determines the values that govern society.

> The church should not just grow wide, but grow deep

I like to put it this way: the church should not just grow wide but grow deep. Growing deep is about influence; growing wide is just numbers but with no real impact.

This brings me to the second paradigm shift that I encountered: the understanding of the Seven Mountains of Influence in the world.

INFLUENCING CULTURE

Have you ever asked yourself why we have several churches in the community and yet the community culture itself has not experienced dramatic transformation as a result?

Any genuine Christian must have pondered on this question.

This is because when we equate the growth of the Kingdom of God to the growth of church gatherings (numerically), we assume because the church is gathering in large numbers, it means the Kingdom is expanding. This is not necessarily the case. In fact, in the Bible the Kingdom grew faster not when the church gathered, but when the church was "scattered" as we read in Acts 8.

The church gathering in large numbers does not equate to influence in the society if the Christians are not intentionally discipling the people within their sphere of influence in the community.

And this can only happen when Christians actively engage in the culture and occupy positions of influence in the society where they can demonstrate and promote the values of the Kingdom.

In other words, the kingdoms of the world will stay in the hands of the devil and the devil does not care if we keep increasing in number, as long as we do not bother to become intentional in discipling people within our spheres of influence in society or try to take over the strategic positions of influence in the marketplace. If we do not intentionally transform the world with the power of the Kingdom, the "perverse world" will soon find its way in our churches and ultimately transform it – and you can see that happening today.

THE MIND MOULDERS OF SOCIETY

In the book Making Jesus Lord by Loren Cunningham (YWAM, 1988, P. 134), Cunningham wrote:

"Sometimes God does something dramatic to get our attention. That is what happened to me in 1975. My family and I were enjoying the peace and quiet of a borrowed cabin in the Colorado Rockies. I was stretched out on a lounge chair in the midday warmth, praying and thinking. I was considering how we Christians not just the mission I was part of, but all of us could turn the world around for Jesus.

A list came to my mind: categories of society, which I believed we should focus on in order to turn nations around to God. I wrote them down and stuck the paper in my pocket.

> The seven mountains are not means for the church to force people into Christianity but to allow the light of Christ to shine where it is most needed

The next day, I met with a dear brother, the leader of Campus Crusade for Christ, Dr. Bill Bright. He shared with me something God had given him — several areas to concentrate on to turn nations back to God! They were the same areas, with different wording here and there, that were written on the page in my pocket. I took it out and showed Bill and we shook our heads in amazement.

Here is the list (refined and clarified a bit over the years) that God gave me that sunny day in Colorado:

The Home; the Church; Schools; Government and Politics; the Media;

Arts, Entertainment and Sports; Commerce, Sciences and Technology.

These sevens spheres of society will help us shape societies for Christ.

An understanding of the Seven Mind Moulders of Society is one of the greatest revelations needed to prepare Christians to extend the Kingdom of God in the marketplace.

The 7 Mountains

Let me begin with these thoughts by Kris Vallotton on how we are to impact the world through the seven mountains.

"There's so much confusion over the revelation of the Seven Mountain Mandate. Often people interpret this language as if the church should take over the world. But nothing could be further from the truth! We are called to SERVE in a way that brings out the best in everyone. Constantine proved that forcing Christianity on everyone was a bad plan and a failed experiment.

Like Joseph and Daniel of the Old Testament who served secular kings, we are called to serve everyone and help them fulfil their divine destiny. Jesus made it clear that people who want to lead or be great must be the servants of all. Serving is the way of leadership in the Kingdom. Forcing our way onto the world is not great leadership." Kris Vallotton (7)

So, as I talk about dominion and taking over the seven mountains of influence, I want to be clear that the primary means through which we do this is by SERVICE; that is serving the world with the resources of a superior Kingdom and letting our light shine and speak for itself. The seven mountains are not means for the church to force people into Christianity but to allow the light of Christ to shine where it is most needed so that men will be drawn to the light of Christ that shines through the Christians in the workplace.

Some people approach the seven mountains mandate as a means to impose Christianity on people; so we assume Christians are to become the owners of all the big businesses, so they can force every employee to attend their church or they will be fired, or Christians are to become Presidents so they can force Christianity on the whole nation. While we seek to gain positions of influence in society, we must remember that ministry is about service; we obtain true dominion by serving not by forcing people to serve us or to be like us.

We must speak up on issues and uphold God's standard in every sphere of life, but it's also equally important that we love everyone no matter their persuasions.

Someday Jesus will rule the world; in the meantime, we should just serve so well and let our good works speak of our Father who loves everyone.

THE CULTURAL MANDATE

In Genesis 1:26-28, God calls all humans, made in His image, to fill the earth with His glory through creating what we commonly call culture. This command in Genesis is commonly referred to by Biblical Scholars as the Cultural Mandate.

The cultural mandate is the command to exercise dominion over the earth, subdue it, and develop its latent potential (Gen. 1:26-28; cf. Gen. 2:15).

The cultural mandate is given to all people. In Genesis 1:26-28, it's given to Adam and Eve as the only people and as representatives of all humanity. In Genesis 9:1 it's given to Noah as the representative of all humanity.

> The cultural mandate is the command to exercise dominion over the earth, subdue it, and develop its latent potential (Gen. 1:26-28; cf. Gen 2:15).

Therefore, the cultural mandate is not just for the people of God. Moreover, it's not uniquely tied to the gospel or the great commission (Matt. 28:18-20), which is a distinct mandate given to the people of God alone.

Having said that, only the true people of God (the church) will be able to fulfil the cultural mandate as it was intended according to the desire to give glory to God. This is why the church must step up and take the leading role in society. The world will continue to be influenced and subdued by humans because that is the mandate God gave to humanity from the beginning.

However, the fallen man will always fall short of God's true standard for how the world should be governed. This where the church comes in with the Gospel to demonstrate to the world a better way: indeed God's way for stewarding the earth in all spheres of influence.

THE MISSION OF GOD'S PEOPLE (8)

"God has created us in his image, so that we may carry out a task, fulfil a mission, pursue a calling," writes Anthony A. Hoekema in his book **Created in God's Image.**

This mission is described in Genesis 1:28:

God blessed them and said to them, Be fruitful and increase in number; fill the earth and subdue it. Rule over the fish in the sea and the birds in the sky and over every living creature that moves on the ground.

This passage, known as the cultural mandate, calls Christians to partner with God in His work. From the very beginning, God planned to entrust the world to humankind. This is what we were made to do.

The calling to work is emphasized again in Genesis 2:15:

The Lord God took the man and put him in the Garden of Eden to work it and take care of it.

Nancy Pearcey writes in her book, **Total Truth:**

Our calling is not just to "go to heaven" but also to cultivate the earth, not just to "save souls" but also to serve God through our work. For God, himself is engaged not only in the work of salvation but also in the work of preserving and developing His creation. When we obey the Cultural Mandate, we participate in the work of God himself.

Our stewardship role is a call for man to work with and for God in everything we do. This is why the Apostle Paul can say,

> *"Whatever you do, work at it with all your heart, as working for the Lord"*
>
> (Colossians 3:23)

The significance of all of our work – in our jobs, our homes, our communities, and our church, is directly related to its connection with God's work.

Pearcey writes: *The lesson of the Cultural Mandate is that our sense of fulfilment depends on engaging in creative, constructive work. The ideal human existence is not eternal leisure or an endless vacation or even a monastic retreat into prayer and meditation but the creative effort expended for the glory of God and the benefit of others.*

Work was instituted before the fall of man; before the need for evangelism. There is an intrinsic value to our work. It is what we do to bring about biblical flourishing, to give others a glimpse of the way things were and are supposed to be.

The Garden of Eden was perfect but not finished. If Adam and Eve had not fallen into sin they would not have stayed in the garden forever. They would have moved out into the world, filling it with God's images and subduing it.

The Hebrew word translated *"subdue"* in verse 28 (Hebrew *kabash*), literally means to make the earth useful for the benefit and enjoyment of human beings. This means we have a responsibility to change whatever is not good; be it suffering, injustice, products and services not working, or policies, and make them something that provides benefits to all.

The idea of the cultural mandate is that God entrusts me with something and He expects me to do something with it, something worthwhile, and something that He finds valuable. This is evident from the very beginning when God placed Adam and Eve on the earth. This calling implies an expectation of human achievement.

This first calling of the biblical story is a calling to the world, a calling that comes for the sake of God's purpose to bless all things that He has made. It is a calling informing and shaping all the people of God throughout the entirety of the Bible.

As Biblical scholar, Michael Williams writes,

Should we miss our first calling, a calling that informs the nature and purpose of our very existence, we will in fact impoverish the biblical portrayal of calling.

THE GREAT COMMISSION AND THE CULTURAL MANDATE (9)

It is undoubtedly significant that the Great Commission follows the Cultural Mandate; without the Fall, there is no need for evangelism. After all, "Missions exists because worship doesn't." There is an urgency to the Great Commission that is for all Christians across all time that requires an all-in attitude. The Gospel must reach the nations, and it must reach them swiftly (Rom. 10:14-15).

> The Cultural Mandate did not end in Genesis, and the Great Commission did not begin in Matthew.

Nevertheless, the Cultural Mandate cannot fade from our missional vision. The Cultural Mandate did not end in Genesis, and the Great Commission did not begin in Matthew. The movement of the canon is one from *creation* to new creation, and the King's Kingdom is one of holistic healing. The restoration of the nations involves worship around the Throne one day, as well as worship in our work and witness this day.

Both the Mandate and the Commission are God-breathed and God-ordained. Both proceed from the mouth of God as His effective and living Word, not to be taken as a mere suggestion. The Mandate and the Commission serve as archetypes for Christian work and witness.

When we pray, *"Your kingdom come; your will be done,"* we are praying for both personal and public restoration. Work is worship because God is a worker. Missions is worship because God is the Messiah.

The Greatest Commandment

The Cultural Mandate and the Great Commission are both expressions of the Greatest Commandment and the second which is like it. *"'Love the Lord your God with all your heart and with all your soul and with all your mind… Love your neighbor as yourself'"* (Matt. 22:37, 39).

We are never more in line with the heart of Jesus than when we are abiding in His love: loving God and neighbour in return.

Our neighbour does not merely need our good works. He needs our vocational work and our Gospel witness. We love God and neighbour by producing quality goods and services; by fighting for the suffering, being concerned about poor and wealth generation, finding solutions to sicknesses and diseases. We love God and neighbour by sharing the Gospel with those who have never heard. We must both demonstrate and

> The revelation of the seven mountains is a practical blueprint of how the original Cultural Mandate of Gen 1:26-28 can be fulfilled in this Kingdom age through the Great Commission with the Greatest Commandment as our guide and modus operandi.

declare the love and grace of our Lord.

The revelation of the seven mountains is a practical blueprint of how the original Cultural Mandate of Genesis 1:26-28 can be fulfilled in this Kingdom age through the Great Commission with the Greatest Commandment as our guide and modus operandi.

As Christians, our work in each of these seven mountains of influences is a continuation of the Cultural Mandate from the beginning, with a new impetus, a new ability, a new reality, a new Commission the Great Commission.

7 NATIONS MIGHTIER THAN THEE (10)

> *"This is how you will know that the living God is among you and that he will certainly drive out 7 enemies before you including the Canaanites, Hittites, Hivites, Perizzites, Girgashites, Amorites and the Jebusites"*
>
> (Joshua 3:10)

> *"When the Lord your God brings you into the land which you go to possess, and has cast out many nations before you, the Hittites*

and the Girgashites and the Amorites and the Canaanites and the Perizzites and the Hivites and the Jebusites, seven nations greater and mightier than thou"

(Deuteronomy 7:1)

In the scriptures above, there is a very clear prophetic picture of how the Israelites were to obtain the Promised Land. This is a picture of how God intends for the church to extend the Kingdom and exercise dominion in the world.

The seven nations mentioned in Deuteronomy and Joshua are synonymous to the seven mountains of society today. Crossing the Jordan of baptism/salvation is not enough; it is not the goal. The goal is to reach the Promised Land of Kingdom influence and dominion in society.

However, as we see in the temptations of Jesus, the Promised Land is not an empty piece of land. It is occupied territory. And the people occupying are not godly. The devil has been actively placing his people at the top of the mountains to rule and serve his purposes. But Jesus came to disarm the devil and ensure God's people can have dominion and propagate God's system of doing things across the world.

This will happen not by the church or Christians targeting physical individuals in order to remove from the positions of power and influence as most Christians who misunderstand the dominion mandate tend to think. This will happen by the church addressing the demonic forces influencing these individuals. These could lead to a change of direction of such individuals and even their conversion, and this can lead to a massive turn around for the Kingdom of God and draw many to Christ.

A good example of this is the story of Kanye West; the popular secular musician who for several years influenced many in the mountain of entertainment through his music; but when he encountered God and got saved, he began using his enormous influence in that domain to draw the attention of many to the gospel – this is the power of influencing a mountain. Dominion is not always about putting "Christians" in positions of power, but also influencing those already in positions of power in a way that draws them closer to God.

However, in some cases, individuals will leave or be removed from certain positions of influence and such opportunities will arise for godly people to fill and propagate the values of the Kingdom of God – when the righteous rule, the people rejoice.

The church's mission is not to be an island where people gather for safety and seclusion from the world; it is rather a training and equipping centre for people who God has called to take the Kingdom to the ends of the world; discipling nations to obey the principles and precepts of the Kingdom of God.

When God wanted to Influence a nation, He placed His servants near the mountain of influence. See examples below

Person	Nation	Leader	Result
Moses	Egypt	Pharaoh	Deliverance/Birth nation
Nehemiah	Babylon	King Artaxerxes	Rebuild wall
Daniel	Babylon	King Neb	Nation Influence
Joseph	Egypt	Pharaoh	Saved a nation
Esther	Persia	King Ahasuerus	Saved a nation

JESUS, LORD OVER ALL DOMAINS OF INFLUENCE (10)

(Not just Lord over salvation)

The following scriptures show us very clearly what God's real purpose is. It is more than just salvation; we are called to be a light to the world, to illuminate our generation.

> "But you are a chosen generation, a royal priesthood, a holy nation, His own special people, that you may proclaim the praises of Him who called you out of darkness into His marvellous light"
>
> (1 Peter 2:9-10)

Marketplace Shift

Let's look at a summary of each of these seven mountains of influence, what they are and what it might look like when Christians are equipped and released to extend the Kingdom of God in each of these domains.

1. The Mountain of FAMILY

Family is defined as parents and their children. It's an institution created by God. Family and morality are the very fibre of order for society. When family order disintegrates, then social order also disintegrates. Societal ills and dysfunctions have coincided with the breakdown of the family unit. Broken homes are major contributors to almost every societal ill imaginable. A family's glue is love. Without love, the family cannot exist.

> The world needs Christians called into the domain of family to help restore broken homes and families

The Jebusite nation rules the family mountain. Jebusite means: trodden down, rejection. Rejection is defined as the refusal to accept, consider, submit to, hear, receive, or admit. Basically, the opposite of love. A person can go through a lifetime of counselling and still not recover from the effects of rejection.

It starts with the parents. He will turn the hearts of the fathers to the children, and the hearts of the children to the fathers (Malachi 4:6). It 'IS' the last verse of the Old Testament. Clearly, families are under assault. At the centre of this problem is the lack of fathers who are fully engaged in the life of their family. But the Lord will come and He will save the families. Father, Lord of the family.

The world needs Christians called into this domain of family to help restore broken homes and families. This can take a variety of ways including working as a social worker, a counsellor, a therapist, a family lawyer, and many other professions where Christians with an understanding of God's blueprint for the family can disciple whole families and communities and help to restore them to the original design and purpose of the family as ordained by God.

I had the opportunity to meet a dear friend of mine Aquiles from Bolivia who runs a ministry dedicated to helping young girls who have been victims of sex trafficking. These young girls have had no practical experience of what it means to be truly loved. All they have ever experienced from men is rejection and abuse. They can only understand the love of God (The Greatest Commandment) when someone can come alongside them and help them come out from the dreadful situation in which they find themselves and provide a safe place for them to regain a sense of dignity and identity. It is from there that they can be able to understand the love of the Father – this is what ministering the Kingdom of God in the Mountain of Family can look like.

There are several examples and cases of brokenness in the domain of family and Christians need to rise and become salt and light in these places of darkness. This is how the Kingdom of God moves into the marketplace.

2. The Mountain of EDUCATION

Education is defined as the activities of teaching or instructing; activities that impart knowledge or skill; knowledge acquired by learning and instruction; the gradual process of acquiring knowledge.

Education is a skill or knowledge received by a learning process. In the world, the mountain of education is dominated by schools such as Harvard, Yale and Princeton... all of which started off as Christian colleges and universities. These top universities, as well as the majority of all other universities and public schools, are dominated by liberal and humanistic philosophies. Our current education systems emphasize the left-brain understanding of truth. Our left-brain dominated curriculum and instruction leaves little room for right-brain development in children and young adults. The right-brain is where we receive creative, imaginative, and in- tuitive revelation from God.

> God should not be pushed out of our classrooms, but rather standing in the front giving the lesson

The education system is turning children into rationalistic and critical thinkers limiting them to the five human senses and thus, preventing them from receiving God's revelation. The Amorites rule the education mountain. Amorites means: to boast, to act proudly, the pride in one's heart, self-exaltation.... the basic thoughts of humanism. Humanism prioritizes human qualities and intellect. The source of humanism can be traced back to Greek philosophy. Spin-offs of humanism are atheism, liberalism, and rationalism.

We need to turn education back to a right-brain dominant curriculum and open the way for children to learn how to hear from God. We need to bring God back into the classroom to make His teachings the foundation for the curriculum. God should not be pushed out of our classrooms, but rather standing in the front giving the lesson. But how will God stand in front of the class to give a lesson? It's by sending Christian teachers into the classroom who carry the revelation and the heart of God for education.

The time has come for the church to equip and release Marketplace Ministers called into the Education Mountain to demonstrate Jesus as the Great Teacher – Lord of Education.

I had the opportunity to meet a dear sister in Christ from Indonesia, Ruth Devi. Ruth has a passion to see a transformation in the education sector in her country. She runs a ministry called New Hope International and her mission is to train teachers in schools on biblical methods and principles of education. This is to enable holistic education that prepares students to be effective and productive members of their community, living lives that honour God. Her ministry affects thousands of teachers in Indonesia and as a result, hundreds of thousands of children are impacted by these teachers.

3. The Mountain of GOVERNMENT

The dictionary defines government as *The political direction and control exercised over the actions of the members, citizens, or inhabitants of communities, societies, and states; the form or system of rule by which a state, community, etc., is governed; the governing body of persons in a state, community, etc.*

This mountain has been completely ignored by the church. Many consider it "of the devil" because of all the corruption and deceit that take place in this arena. Unfortunately, since the church has chosen to ignore this mountain the enemy has easily moved in and taken over.

The Girgashites rule on the mountain of government. Girgashites translated means earthly. It represents being motivated by earthly desires. Pride often is the driving force that leads to many Politician's feeling they are beyond accountability. The desire for the riches of this earth ends in corruption and immorality.

Pride was the reason Lucifer was cast out of Heaven. One can see the influence of the devil in our politics. Not all politicians are 'of the devil.' But in general, politics is dominated by greed, corruption, immorality and pride: all the tools of satan. But God has said that He will displace satan and expose all his lies. The time has come for us to take back our governments and to place Jesus at the top.

The time has come for the church to equip and release Marketplace Ministers called into Government Mountain to demonstrate Jesus as the King of Kings and the Lord of Justice.

In 2019, I had the privilege to visit the South African House of Parliament in Cape Town and was pleased to meet a member of parliament who is a devoted and committed Christian and who through his influence and that of other Christians in parliament (even as minorities) have been able to cause a change in the policies of the government and have championed the fight against corruption in the government, with amazing results. What amazed me was how much faith they had in God's ability to use them to bring transformation in government; their fearlessness in the face of even death threats and their confidence in the fact that their work in government is a ministry unto God. They, like Daniel, are not afraid for their lives because they know they are on God's side and because of that they know they are the majority.

I also had the privilege to meet a dear friend from Kenya, Kimone Kimone (Philip) who through his engagement with the political landscape of his country is bringing transformation in the government and influencing government policies; creating enabling environment for job creation and empowerment for the youth in Kenya.

4. The Mountain of ECONOMY

The economy is the proper flow and balance of the production of resources, distribution, and consumption of resources. An economy is healthy when there's a proper relationship between these three elements. The world economy is influenced and controlled by world money traders who create economic realities. These traders determine a nation's economic health and determine the value of that nation's currency. If man, can determine the value of a nation's economic worth, then the enemy can manipulate it and influence the outcome.

The Canaanites rule the Economy Mountain (also referred to as the Business Mountain). Canaanite in Hebrew can be translated as merchant, trader, and trafficker, along with *'to be humbled, brought low or to be under subjection'*. The word Cana means zealous. Together, these words paint a picture of greed and poverty.

God is Jehovah-Jireh, which means *"the Lord is my provider."* God's heart is for every person and every nation to live under His provision. He delights in providing for His children. Money and resources are a blessing from God. The zeal for those resources is the root of all kinds of evil. Money itself is not evil or good. Money is simply a tool. The enemy has convinced everyone that money is their true source of provision. His goal is to enslave people to poverty, where God blesses with abundance. The enemy twists God's abundance into greed for more.

> The time has come for the church to equip and release Marketplace Ministers called into the Economic Mountain to demonstrate Jesus as Jehovah Jireh – Lord of Economics

The economic systems of this world are going to collapse; which is a good thing as it will leave people with nothing or no one to turn to except for God. God calls His people to come out of the world's system, out of poverty, out of the idea that money is our provision and into His system of abundance and provision.

I love the story of Graham Power, whom I was privileged to meet in South Africa in 2019 when he came to teach in our class.

How do you go from strangling a nation through corruption, and then be assigned by God to eradicate corruption throughout the world? That's the story of Graham Power.

Working in construction since 18, Graham started The Power Group at the age of 28. By the age of 43, his firm was linked with other construction leaders in price-fixing, bid-rigging, and other practices that strangled commercial and government construction projects throughout South Africa. All of that changed in a single night – alone in his study.

God changed Graham's life, his business, and his priorities.

Graham Power became the founder of Unashamedly Ethical a global movement engaging leaders to pledge themselves to accountably honest living; bringing business leaders and government leaders into honest and ethical practices throughout the world a campaign to challenge the culture of corruption in Africa and beyond.

"Power Group" (www.powergrp.co.za) is one of Africa's leading construction firms.

Marketplace Shift

The time has come for the church to equip and release Marketplace Ministers called into Economic Mountain to demonstrate Jesus as Jehovah Jireh Lord of Economics.

5. The Mountain of COMMUNICATION

The communication (media) mountain consists of TV channels, newspapers, magazines, radio, and Internet sites any media outlet that reports the news. We have never really recognized the power of the media. However, the advent of the internet and social media has demonstrated the immense power of the media.

The media can create news. They can take a minor event and turn it into a big story or take a big event and turn it into a minor story. Many times, news stories are driven by the type of ratings they will produce or the agenda of the owners. Scandals and bad news seem to dominate the airways. The enemy has occupied this mountain for too long. The Hittite Nation rules the media mountain.

Hittite translated means fear or terror or to destroy. The reality is terrorists would be a lot less effective if the press didn't give them so much coverage. The news stories about the terrorist are actually causing more fear and terror than the terrorists themselves.

> The Christians reporting the news will become the new evangelists

The Hittite nation was large and

expansive, much like the media mountain. The Internet alone seems to have no limit, and television is wired into almost every household.

The goal for the media mountain is to report the news accurately, regardless if it's bad or good news. The people reporting the news will speak to the hearts of the viewers or readers and have the ability to affect them all positively, regardless of the nature of the story. They will become the new evangelists.

The time has come for the church to equip and release Marketplace Ministers called into Communication Mountain to demonstrate Jesus as the Living Word Lord of Communication.

6. The Mountain of CELEBRATION

The Celebration Mountain is also referred to as the Arts and Entertainment Mountain.

This mountain includes arts, music, sports, fashion, entertainment and every other way we celebrate or enjoy life. This mountain, like that of government, is so captured by satan that most Christians don't feel it can be taken back or if it even should be. IT ABSOLUTELY MUST BE TAKEN BACK!!! This is the gateway to the youth. For a large part of a young person's life, this is the only mountain they care about. Satan cannot be allowed to have a free run at our young. This mountain is where creativity shows up and God is in the business of creating. Satan cannot create, he can only counterfeit.

> Every form of art, sport, music, literature, movies and any other form of celebration needs to be produced God's way by being in His presence and letting His creativity flow through them

The Hivite Nation rules the Arts and Entertainment Mountain. Their name means villagers and life-giving place. These are the enemy villagers who are occupying a life-giving place. They represent counterfeit, deception, and perversion. Our first encounter with a Hivite (in Genesis 34:1-2) was a rape of one of the daughters of Jacob. They pervert and misinterpret what is supposed to be a blessing. They deceive what was meant for good (i.e...sex) to appear to be evil so it will be rejected by God's people.

God's Spirit wants to move freely through the creativity and passion of God's people.

Every form of art, sport, music, literature, movies and any other form of celebration needs to be produced God's way by being in His presence and letting His creativity flow through them. We must help everyone see through the deception of our pop culture and reveal the truth. We must provide real and lasting alternative forms of celebration.

The only way to successfully reclaim these mountains is with prayer and action. Prayer by itself will not accomplish it and action by itself will not accomplish it. Only through a combined effort will these mountains be taken for the Kingdom. Potter, Lord of the Arts & Beauty.

In 2019, we saw the power of this mountain with the conversion of Kanye West. I mentioned this earlier. Those who lead this mountain have a tremendous influence on the youth.

7. The Mountain of RELIGION

The religion mountain (also known as the church mountain) is probably the most obvious of the mountains, and the one we are most familiar with. We have filled the mountain with people, but these people have not been properly trained or equipped to carry out the mission. Religion is defined as "the service and worship of God, or the supernatural."

We have learned a lot about religion in a negative context as that which is ritual and not real, but there is a pure and undefiled religion that is good. There are over 2.1 billion followers of Christ, which is more than the next two combined (Islam and Hinduism).

Christianity is the fastest-growing religion in the world, and their numbers and influence are growing exponentially. That is a vast army just waiting to take back the mountain.

The Perizzites rule the Church Mountain. Perizzites means without walls, rustic dweller.

Unwalled denotes that they have no protection and rustic dwellers means they experience limited provision. In scripture, idolatry was entrenched in the high places, the last holdouts in Israel's struggles against false worship. Idolatry strips people of their protection and their provision.

Idolatry is particularly deceptive because the very thing it causes, which is death and lack, are the very things it pretends to cure. This mountain can only be taken through the dynamic leading and power of the Holy Spirit. All who will penetrate this mountain must commit to be true worshipers. This charge must be on the back of true worship. Worship in spirit and in truth is passionate, abandoned, radical worship. It is not three hymns or songs and a prayer. Freedom in worship and an increase in the Holy Spirit anointing are a direct cause-and-effect that cannot be ignored. These warriors will have supernatural experiences with God that defies the expectations and traditions of status quo Christianity.

These seven mountains are not exhaustive but are a practical guide to help Christians identify the domains where God is calling them to extend the Kingdom of God. For each mountain, there are diverse professions and careers which Christians can be called into; each with a unique gift mix, talents and anointing to influence the culture in these mountains for the expansion of the Kingdom of God.

REFLECTION QUESTIONS

1. As we have seen in this chapter, the original mandate (the cultural mandate) given to all mankind was to have dominion and govern the earth for the glory of God. In what ways has mankind succeeded in accomplishing this command? In what ways has mankind failed?

2. The great commission and the cultural mandate are two sides of the same coin. How do you see yourself fulfilling both the cultural mandate and the great commission in your sphere of influence?

3. The seven spheres of influences are a guide to areas where the Lord wants His Kingdom to reign; how do you see the Lord reigning through you in your sphere of influence?

CHAPTER SUMMARY

1. The Cultural Mandate
-The cultural mandate is the command to exercise dominion over the earth, subdue it, and develop its latent potential (Gen. 1:26-28; cf. Gen. 2:15).

2. The Great Commission
-The Great Commission follows the Cultural Mandate; without the Fall, there is no need for evangelism.

3. The Greatest Commandment
-The Cultural Mandate and the Great Commission are both expressions of the Greatest Commandment and the second which is like it: "'Love the Lord your God with all your heart and with all your soul and with all your mind… Love your neighbour as yourself'" (Matt. 22:37, 39).

4. The Seven Mountains of Culture/Influence
- The revelation of the seven mountains is a practical blueprint of how the original Cultural Mandate of Genesis 1:26-28 can be fulfilled in this Kingdom age through the Great Commission with the Greatest Commandment as our guide and modus operandi.
-Family, Education, Government, Economy, Communication, Celebration and Religion.

Chapter Six

CHURCH SHIFT
A Shift in How We Do Church

"I give you the name Peter, a stone. And this truth of who I am will be the bedrock foundation on which I will build my church my legislative assembly, and the power of death will not be able to overpower it!"

Matthew 16:18 (The Passion Translation)

CHURCH SHIFT
A Shift in How We Do Church

IN Matthew 16:18 when Jesus introduced the church, He used some very strong and specific words to describe it. I like to quote this scripture from the Message Bible Translation.

You are Peter, a rock. This is the rock on which I will put together my church, a church so expansive with energy that not even the gates of hell will be able to keep it out. (Matthew 16:18)

THE ECCLESIA

The word *"church"* in Matthew 16:8 comes from the word "Ecclesia" and this word is not a religious word. It is a very political and governmental word.

The Ecclesia is a gathering of citizens convened from their homes into a public place to deliberate.

This is different from a synagogue which was the building where the Jews gathered to listen to their religious leaders read from the scriptures.

By its very nature, the Ecclesia is a law-making body, whose mission is to deliberate on affairs concerning the society that the Ecclesia represents.

> The Ecclesia is a gathering of citizens convened from their homes into a public place for deliberating.

Closely followed in Matthew 16:9, Jesus gives a perfect example of the power of this new legislative body as far as the Kingdom of God is concerned.

"I will give you the keys of Heaven's kingdom realm to forbid on earth that which is forbidden in heaven, and to release on earth that which released in heaven"

(Matthew 16:9)

It's important to note here where the focus of the power and keys are directed. They are directed towards the earth (the world). The church has the mandate to release Heaven on earth and at the same time stopping and bringing to nought all the activities and operations of the enemy wherever it may be found. And Jesus said this body, this ecclesia is so full and expansive with energy that no gate of hell can STOP its advancement.

> The gates of hell is not coming against the church. The church is going against the gates of hell.

Marketplace Shift

The gates of hell are not coming against the church. The church is going against the gates of hell. It's important to adopt the right posture.

OUT OF THE BOX

Ever since the fourth century when the Roman Emperor Constantine made Christianity legal, the church progressively went from a decentralized *"saints movement"* to a temple-centred, *"clergy-dependent"* movement.

We went from focusing on marketplace presence to building elaborate cathedrals with clergy-led rituals/services. We went from people "being the church" to people "going to church." I call the latter mentality "the box church."

This clergy/laity divide and emphasis with a ritual-centred approach in a building was not only a challenge in the past but also in the present. Consequently, the leaders of the church held a monopoly upon things sacred which kept the "holy elite" in power and wealth. The sad thing is, similar concepts are still prevalent in the church today. This is a mindset that must change if the church must experience real Kingdom advancement in the marketplace.

The following are some of the contrasts between the *"Box Church"* And *"Kingdom-Centred" Church.*

The Box Church vs Kingdom-Centred Church (11)

The box church Christians go to church. The kingdom-centred Christians are the church. Whenever we say, *"We are going to church,"* it shows we are still trapped within the mindset that the church is primarily a building we go to.

The box church focuses most of its energy into the Sunday experience in a building. The kingdom-centred church equips Christians for Monday to Friday. *The kingdom-centred church not only has a good Sunday experience but also equips the saints for the work of the ministry related to their primary vocation from Monday to Friday.*

In the box church, only the professional clergy are ministers. In the kingdom-centred church, all Christians are equipped to minister for God.

In the box church, only the clergy can understand the Word. The kingdom-centred church equips all Christians to interpret and apply the Word.

In the box church, people are taught to be dependent upon the *"man of God"* to feed them the Word. In the kingdom-centred church, the focus is to teach all Christians to interpret the Word and feed themselves.

> Whenever we say, "We are going to church", it shows we are still trapped within the mind-set that the church is primarily a building we go to.

In the box church, potential leaders are equipped to preach in a building. The kingdom-centred church equips people to lead in the marketplace.

Marketplace Shift

In the box church, a small percentage of people with potential are trained to become full-time clergy and preach the Word. In the kingdom-centred church, the focus is on equipping one hundred percent of the people to influence culture through their vocation.

In the box church, only Sunday is celebrated and sacred. In the kingdom-centred church, every day is celebrated and sacred. *In kingdom-centred churches, every day is viewed as a sacred opportunity to demonstrate the love, wisdom, and power of God in all of life.*

In the box church, the real mission is Sunday. In the kingdom-centred church, the real mission is Monday to Friday.

In the box church, the people are trained to try to make it to Sunday to get eNcouraged and filled. In the kingdom-centred church, the Sunday service equips the believer to bring the lordship of Christ to every facet of society.

> The kingdom-centered church not only has a good Sunday experience but also equips the saints for the work of the ministry related to their primary vocation from Monday to Friday

In the box church, wealth creators are only used for their tithe/offerings to support programs in a building. In the kingdom-centred church, wealth creators use their business to advance the kingdom in culture.

In the box church, the temple is the sanctuary. In the kingdom-centred church, the earth is His sanctuary. The Scriptures say t*hat the earth is the Lord's and the fullness thereo*f (Ps. 24). *Hence, we should experience the activity of God as much in city hall as we do the fellowship hall inside a church building.*

The box church depends upon a building to function. The kingdom-centred church depends on Christians to function.

In the box church, ministry is limited or expanded by the capacity of their building. In the kingdom-centred church, the ministry is limited or expanded by the capacity of the disciples they are equipping and sending.

In the box church, Jesus is only the saviour of the sheep. In the kingdom-centred church, Jesus is also the King of kings over nations. In the kingdom-centred church, saved people view Jesus as the President of all presidents, the CEO of all CEOs, and the Judge of all lawyers and judges of the earth (Rev. 19:16). Hence, they speak truth to power as God's representatives.

> The kingdom-centered church views every day as a sacred opportunity to demonstrate the love, wisdom and power of God in all of life.

In the box church, the Bible is a book about escaping the earth. In the kingdom-centred church, the Bible is about stewarding the earth. The Bible is the most practical book ever written about how to live upon the earth. Hence, *the biblical focus is for Christians to experience inner transformation so they can transform their surrounding culture (internal transformation without external goals of engagement results in narcissism and passivity).*

The box church focuses on bringing the community into a building. The kingdom-centred church focuses on sending the saints to serve their city.

In the box church, the gifts of the Spirit operate on Sunday. In the kingdom-centred church, the gifts of the Spirit operate every day.

> The Bible is the most practical book ever written about how to live upon the earth. Hence, the biblical focus is for Christians to experience inner transformation so they can transform their surrounding culture

In the box church, our purpose began when we were born again. In the kingdom-centred church, our purpose was evident immediately after physical birth. *God's purpose for us was in motion even before we were saved since He anoints and sanctifies our God-given natural gifts, talents, and past worldly experience to advance His kingdom.*

In the box church, people come to be entertained. In the kingdom-centred church, people come to be equipped.

In the box church, the lead pastor is called to shepherd a congregation. In the kingdom-centred church, the lead pastor is called to shepherd a community.

The box church is mystical. The kingdom-centred church is spiritual. *The biblical use of the word "spiritual" does not necessarily mean thinking of spiritual things—but it has to do with having power over your flesh to be a witness of Christ on the earth. Hence, mysticism and biblical spirituality imply two different things; mysticism implies spirituality with no practical application to the earth while true spirituality empowers us to deal with earthly realities.*

In the box church, Christians come to escape their problems. In the kingdom-centred church, they learn how to become problem solvers.

In the box church, people passively wait to be caught up into heaven. In the kingdom-centred church, we bring heaven down to the earth. *Jesus told us to pray for His kingdom to come on earth as it is in heaven (Matt. 6:10). He prayed that we would not be taken out of the world (John 17:15). He told us to occupy or engage in business until He comes (Luke 19:13).*

> God's purpose for us was in motion even before we were saved, since He anoints and sanctifies our God-given natural gifts, talents and past worldly experience to advance His kingdom.

THE PURPOSE OF THE POWER AND THE KEYS

At the beginning of this book, I emphasised the importance of us understanding the Gospel of the Kingdom before the church. This is because, without this understanding, the powers given to the legislative body (the church/ecclesia) will not be used for its intended purpose. Let me illustrate:

Imagine a new country was being set-up in a new territory. For the country to run smoothly, it needs an assembly in which its citizens can be represented to deliberate on issues that concern the nation. The assembly exists to serve the purpose of the nation and its citizens. The assembly has very strong powers to make laws and define how the nation is governed.

However, imagine if the members of the assembly were to devote all their energy and time to themselves; what do you think will happen to the nation? Let me give you an illustration of what I think will happen

Firstly, the members will focus on building a better house of assembly where they can meet in greater comfort and security.

They will be more concerned about their wellbeing: how much benefits they receive each time they gather in their assembly meetings.

They might not be very current about the issues affecting the different communities and localities of the nation because they are not really concerned about anything that happens outside the house of assembly.

Imagine if the members of the assembly tell the rest of the nation that, the only way they can benefit from the resources of the nation is if they come to the house of assembly. This will be very wrong of them.

However, if each time the assembly gathers, the members spend time discussing issues that affect the nation and begin deliberating on solutions that can improve the general well-being of the nation, the entire nation will directly feel the impact of this assembly. In a typical democratic society, if the members of the assembly are not doing anything to address the challenges of the nation, they will be voted out.

The Kingdom of God is like the whole nation; the church is the legislative assembly of the Kingdom. Its purpose is to serve the mission of the Kingdom of God which is to rule society based on the principles and culture of Heaven.

Any legislative assembly that does not perform its functions to serve the nation and its citizen has lost its relevance (*when salt loses its taste*) and will be voted out of power

> The church is the legislative assembly of the Kingdom. Its purpose is to serve the mission of the Kingdom of God, which is to rule society based on the principles and culture of Heaven

(trampled upon by men).

Scripture says we are the salt of the earth and when salt loses its taste, it will be trampled upon by men (Matt. 5:13).

With this understanding, the church should have a different focus on how it measures its growth and effectiveness.

Now, the analogy I just gave is not a word-for-word description of how the church should operate. However, it gives a general orientation on how we should evaluate the church's impact on society.

All the powers and keys granted to the church was not meant for the church itself, but the expansion of the Kingdom of God. The difference is the Kingdom expands as citizens of the Kingdom of God (who are also members of the Ekklesia) are released into the nation (society) to disciple the culture and change it to reflect the culture and ways of Heaven.

CRUISE SHIP OR BATTLESHIP

In chapter one, I introduced the paradigm shift that needs to happen in our understanding and approach to church. This paradigm is based on a renewed understanding of the gospel, which is about extending the Kingdom of God and not just about individual salvation of souls.

One of the most striking illustrations the Lord gave me about how the church needs to shift for the Kingdom to advance in the marketplace was to use the difference between a cruise ship and a battleship.

A Cruise ship is designed for entertainment. A Battleship is equipped for war.

> A Cruise ship is designed for entertainment. A Battleship is equipped for war.

I will start by using two scenarios to illustrate this:

A Cruise ship scenario and a Battleship scenario

Cruise Ship Church Growth Scenario

The church (missionaries) enters a city or community; look for a good location or hall and begin preparing to invite and receive people who want to experience what the church offers. We invest in making the place as comfortable and welcoming as possible, so people can have a great experience when they come to church. We win souls, disciple people, and encourage them to bring more people to come and experience this new church. As we continue to do this, people come and have a great experience and some stay and the church continues to grow. While this is good and shows that the church is growing; there is still little evidence of the impact of the church in that community.

A Personal Experience

In the course of writing this book, I was carrying out a study of the com-

munity where I live. I met one of the eldest members of this community and asked him about the challenges that this community has been facing over the years. After narrating the different challenges; I asked him the question "How have Christians been involved in solving these community problems?" His answer was very shocking. He said the Christians are simply churchgoers. He said the Christians are just contented with going to church but after church, they simply forget the message they hear in church and go about their lives without any concern for the challenges of the community. He actually said most of them are just self-centred, only interested in enriching themselves and do not really care about the community as a whole.

If the church is supposed to be salt and light in a community, it must be Kingdom-oriented. Remember the church is the legislative assembly of the Kingdom of God and has as its primary mission, the extension of the realities of the Kingdom into the wider community and not just within the gathering of its members.

Battleship Church Growth Scenario

The church (missionaries) enters a city or community; look at the state of the community; identify the challenges of the communities and deliberates on ways to bring the Kingdom of God into this community to address the needs of the community. As the assembly deliberates, they identify that there is high delinquency in the region, unemployment, lack of potable water, etc. The church begins a project to address these needs; maybe start a vocational training centre to train the youths on some practical life skills or start a potable water project for the community. This initiative already opens a door for the church to begin impacting the city.

Through this initiative, as the youths gain practical skills, as the community benefits from the portable *water (brought in by the church)*, the Holy Spirit is at work ministering to their spiritual and social needs through the Christians who are running the project. As people begin to encounter God, a fellowship grows naturally from it and a new assembly is created where new converts are trained to carry out similar kingdom invasion missions in other communities. By the time this initiative is advanced, other aspects of the community will be gradually transformed as the church begins to lunch more interventions to address other needs in the community; family, education, government, arts, sports, and in all spheres of life. The result is that unemployment goes down, delinquency reduces, and the general well-being of the community improves as the church brings the Kingdom of God into the whole community.

This is a holistic approach that addresses every facet of society and not only the souls of people which is the result when the gospel of salvation is the primary focus of the church.

What happens when the church takes this approach?

The church will become the main provider of all social, economic, spiritual, and other amenities in the community. The sports centres/gyms will be run by the church (by church, I am not referring to the "institution of the church" but the people, the Christians.) In other words, the businesses in the community will be mostly run by Christians; the sports/gyms, the schools, the hospitals, the councils, the government agencies, etc. will be run by Christian (who are agents and representatives of the Kingdom of God).

The general assembly where Christians gather will no longer be the only place for people of the community to encounter God. The whole community will be infused with God's presence as Gods' people take up positions of influence in the whole community. In this case, you can truly say the church has indeed left the building. This requires a total radical mind shift in the way we do church.

THE KINGDOM NEEDS A BATTLESHIP CHURCH

For the Kingdom of God to advance in the marketplace, we need a radical paradigm shift in how we do church. This might come as a challenge to many Christians and particularly Church leaders. Like I said in chapter one, we cannot pour new wine in old wineskin. Advancing the Kingdom in the marketplace is not just about encouraging people in the church to do business; the whole system of doing church must change.

You cannot transform a Cruise Ship into a Battleship by simply making some cosmetic adjustments. That is putting new wine in old wineskin; the Bible makes it clear it will not work.

Our Cruise Ship church model has been great at gathering people and giving them a great experience in the building. However, it has not been effective at releasing these people to change the world around them. In fact, if we look at the most outstanding churches today, even the impact they have created in the community has been greatly driven by the church leadership itself. The greater crowd is still very much ineffective at changing their own communities and spheres of influence where they find themselves.

It is one thing to have a church which has a great building on large acres of land, offering different facilities and amenities where people need to come from far and wide to experience it; and it is another thing to have members of the church across the world creating impact and changing the lives of people in the different localities where they find themselves.

The first approach is the Cruise Ship model and the results are outstanding and amazing. However, it's not enough for Kingdom expansion and dominance in the world. I believe the battleship model will see the church as an institution still develop great structures but with a totally different mind-set. This mind-set is not for people to come and see the wonders of what God is doing in a particular building, but to come and be equipped to bring transformation in their different spheres of influence.

The Cruise Ship attracts, but the Battleship advances and conquers new territories for the Kingdom. The Cruise Ship wants a place to settle and wait for people to come to it. With the Battleship, we are not looking for a place to settle, we are looking for a community to transform and make it look like Heaven.

BEYOND CHURCH GROWTH TO KINGDOM EXPANSION (12)

There was an era when the focus was on Church Growth the church growth movement. I believe we are in a new era where the new focus is on Kingdom Expansion. And this two are not exactly the same.

Positive Contributions of Church Growth Movement

The church growth movement caused us to look seriously at the mission or purpose of the church and to ask whether we are actually fulfilling that mission.

The church growth movement challenged us to look at the effectiveness or the health of the church. We were forced to look at the statistical evidence and ask the hard questions. Are we growing? Are we making a difference?

It required us to look at the components of effective churches such as leadership, small groups, homogeneity, receptivity, and worship style.

It required the pastor and/or staff to look at their leadership style and ask about effectiveness.

We were forced to ask questions about "relevance" in terms of whether we were actually communicating effectively to those sitting in our pews and those we were trying to reach.

We were challenged to think about the different age groupings in terms of their learning styles and preferences. Thus, we had books and conferences on church growth. These contributed to a greater sensitivity in both ministry and outreach.

The church growth movement has certainly taught us and challenged us to look, evaluate, think, and change. But when we are forced to ask the hard question has it produced substantial results in terms of "growth?" has it produced substantial results in terms of our impact in the society (world)? has it produced results in terms of how much the culture has been transformed by the Gospel? Most have generally concluded that it has not done so. I asked a question in the first chapter, why do we have more churches and yet we still have a much more corrupt society?

The main reason why the church has not had as much impact in the society (world) as it ought to is that, in emphasising church growth, we have also emphasised only the ministries that happen in and to the church; and have not developed and promoted the ministries directed towards the society/world.

The Downside of the Church Growth Movement

I believe that certain aspects of the church growth movement led to a theological compromise. The question asked was, "does it work" rather than "does it please God." When one looks at the large numbers of people who are reported as joining churches today just by "professing to be born again," we must ask whether we have been willing to compromise our understanding of believer's faith for growth statistics.

The Kingdom is not just about getting people "saved" and added to a church. It is discipling peoples and nations to live according to Kingdom principles in all spheres of life.

Much of our thinking became "mechanical" in terms of church growth. We began to seek the right method or strategy, depending on "it" to grow our church, rather than expecting God to fulfil His promise to grow His church, while we focus on extending the Kingdom of God and discipling nations.

It often led to the *"cloning of models"* rather than the application of principles. We look for effective models and try to plug them into our church without due consideration of our context, gift mix, history, and heritage and God's Kingdom mission for the church. So many pastors look at the churches that are "growing" and try to replicate their methods to grow their churches.

It often bred a spirit of competition rather than a strategy of cooperation. This "myopic" vision impacted both pew and pulpit. As we "marketed" the church, people wanted to know "what's in it for me." Pastors, in turn, often focused on "growing my church" and ignored co- operative strategies that can extend the Kingdom in a whole wider community; in other words ministry to the world/society as a whole. Decisions were made based on "what's in it for me or my church" rather than "what can we do together for the Kingdom and the World?"

In some cases, the church growth movement bred a CEO mentality among pastors and led to a lack of pastoral concern that saw the laity in terms of "what they can do or provide" to help me grow my church.

> In emphasizing on church growth without kingdom expansion, we have emphasized only the ministries that happen in and to the church; and have not developed and promoted the ministries directed towards transforming the society/world.

The greatest practical weakness of the church growth movement was that it prioritized the least significant issue in terms of church health. It suggested that we needed to change structure, style, or strategy to see the church grow.

We assumed that the only thing that mattered was the (numerical) growth of the church, but neglected the fact that the church's mission is not to grow itself. The church grows to effectively fulfil its mission in the world. Church growth is to be a means to an end and not an end itself the end is Kingdom expansion and cultural transformation.

If you attempt to change one of these elements first, you will generally split the church. While some or all of these elements may need to be changed, we must first change the affection of the church. The heart of the church must be changed so that the passion of the church is to please the King and be used by Him in His Kingdom activity – which is expanding God's Kingdom influence across the city and nation in every sphere of life. This will lead to a change in thinking which will, in turn, allow us to evaluate and change the church structure where necessary.

It is this understanding that will give us the blueprint on how to change the current cruise ship paradigm of church and introduce the battleship paradigm of how we do church.

From Church Growth to Kingdom Expansion

As a pastor, my greatest desire is to see the church reach its full potential here on earth. And for that to happen, there must be a radical shift and rethinking of how we do church in this day and age.

It is true that in this day and age, there has been a lot of attack on the church and that has made many Christians become very defensive and protective of the (their) church and whenever anyone brings up a topic that might speak negatively about the church in the slightest way, a wall is automatically erected.

But let's remember: sometimes criticism causes us to re-evaluate ourselves and find what we might be doing wrong so we can correct and be better.

The church as a body needs to move to the next level of Kingdom expansion: a church that does not focus more on itself but a church that focuses on God's Kingdom invading the world.

How will the church look like when we embrace this paradigm shift? What will the focus of the church?

DIFFERENCE BETWEEN A CRUISE SHIP AND BATTLESHIP CHURCH

Cruise Ship Church	Battleship (Kingdom) Church
Focus on gathering, entertaining and keeping people.	Focus on gathering, equipping and sending people.
Measures impact by how many people it keeps.	Measures impact by how many people it sends.
Measures impact by the number of its people.	Measures impact by the capacity of its people.
Grows big in order to accommodate more people.	Grows big in order to train more people.
Creates & attracts more members and followers.	Creates & attracts more disciples and leaders.
Focus is on the building where people gather.	Focus is on the reason why people gather.
Focus is on creating a great atmosphere in the church building	Focus is on exporting the great atmosphere from the church building

Invests more in equipping the building.	Invests more in equipping the people.
Leaders spent more time trying to make people stay/happy.	Leaders spend more time trying to make people productive/work.
Focuses on church growth at the expense of Kingdom Expansion.	Focuses on Kingdom Expansion resulting in church growth.
Focuses on building its community only.	Focuses on transforming other communities, not just its own.
Focuses on becoming popular in society; in order to attract more people.	Focuses on creating impact in society; attracting more people as a result.

Jesus, John the Baptist, and the apostles went about proclaiming the kingdom; not the church (read Matthew 3:2, 4:17, 10:7; Acts 28:30-31). Although the church is in the kingdom, it is not the entire kingdom.

"Kingdom" denotes the rule of God over the whole cosmos, not just a single entity on the earth, like the church. Despite this, most preaching today has as its goal to get people to make a weekly two-hour commitment to come to a building on Sundays and to give tithes to support that building! This is because a spirit of religion has captivated the church and blinded the minds of church leaders so that we now have a very limiting church mind-set instead of a kingdom perspective. The negative results of this cannot be overstated.

In essence, a kingdom mindset regards Christianity as a biblical world and life view centred on the person of Jesus Christ who is Lord of all creation. This has vast political, economic, and sociological implications! Those with a church mindset view Jesus merely as the King of the church, not the King of all earthly secular kings.

There is a need for a radical mind shift in how we do church if we must see the influence of the Kingdom of God in the wider world and marketplace.

As a Pastor or Church Leader, there are so many things you can do to create a shift in your congregation and begin supporting and developing the ministry of your members for kingdom impact in the marketplace.

The very first step is surely to commit yourself before God to raise them for the work that God has called them into!

In Bethel Church where I am, we began with a ministry focussed on equipping and activating Christians in the workplace (marketplace ministers) for Kingdom expansion. We gather marketplace ministers within the church to meet for fellowship, prayer, and encouragement.

POINTS TO PONDER

I would encourage you to study some of the excellent resources on the Church in the marketplace by Ed Silvoso, Graham Power, Jim Harris, Lance Walnau and Os Hillman.

Here are a few basic steps to begin equipping your members for ministry in the marketplace:

Pray for your Marketplace Ministers

Get the names and business names of the marketplace ministers in your congregation and begin to pray for them and their businesses. Pray for their employees and their families and ask God to deepen their relationship with Him.

Develop your Marketplace Ministers

Very few churches intentionally work to develop and support their marketplace ministers for ministry in the workplace. Start by helping them discover their gifts. Next, help them to connect their gifts and abilities to what they are already doing or facing each day. Pray with them, listen to them and help them to discern God's call for their lives. Then find ways to equip them with the knowledge and skill they will need to fulfil God's calling in their workplace.

Visit your Marketplace Ministers at Work

Make time to visit your marketplace ministers on "their turf." Go there with one simple intention to bless them. Try to sustain this pastoral discipline amid the demands of your ministry. You will not be sorry! As you visit, ask God to show you things about the people, the systems and the place that He wants His Kingdom established. This will enable you to pray "on-site with insight".

Recognise and Celebrate God's Work in the Marketplace

Begin to share the testimonies of what God is doing through the marketplace ministers in your congregation. Regularly, commission marketplace ministers in your church services as missionaries and ministers in the marketplace.

Bless your Marketplace Ministers

Finally, get your congregation behind the ministries of the marketplace ministers. Most often the flow is in the opposite direction: from the marketplace into the congregation.

Commit to shifting from being a pastor to your church only, to being a pastor to your community as well. You won't regret it.

REFLECTION QUESTIONS

Why did God create the Christian Church?

What is the mission of the local church in a community?

What role and function should a pastor or minister fulfil in the community?

How could you encourage and support your pastor to be more supportive of marketplace ministers?

CHAPTER SUMMARY

1. The Church as the Ecclesia

2. The Box Church vs the Kingdom-Centred Church

3. The Cruise Ship vs the Battleship Church

4. From Church Growth to Kingdom Expansion

Chapter Seven

KINGS AND PRIESTS
The Identity of Marketplace Ministers

"And hast made us unto our God kings and priests: and we shall reign on the earth."

(Revelation 5:10 KJV)

7

KINGS AND PRIESTS
The Identity of Marketplace Ministers

I CANNOT end this book, without touching on a very critical and important subject which is very necessary for the activation of Christians in the workplace. In the previous chapters, I have shared the paradigm shifts that must take place for Christians to be activated for Kingdom Expansion in the workplace and all spheres of influence.

However, there is one major requirement that must be emphasised. This is the understanding of the Christians Kingly and Priestly roles in the world today.

THE ROLES OF KINGS AND PRIESTS (13)

The Bible describes two distinct roles for the Old Testament kings and priests: kings were the rulers; priests were the religious leaders. The New Testament reveals we all are kings and priests because of the redemptive work of Christ.

Let's begin by defining each term.

Kings and Priests

A king (basileus) is a person who is a leader of the people, prince, commander, lord of the land.

A priest (hiereus) is one who offers sacrifices in general and fully devoted to Christ alone.

Today, kings are most often represented by business and political leaders, while pastors represent the priestly roles.

Among the greatest of all the enemy's deception is the complete separation of these two roles into clergy and laity. These roles have unfortunately been transformed into and embraced as heavenly truth – that priests and kings are to be always and totally separated; with kings playing a subservient "laymen/laity" role within the kingdom and the priests, the "anointed/clergy" role.

Such a deceptive distinction severely severs the potential supernatural unity and power that can flow between and within kings and priests to transform marketplaces and nations to fund the end-time harvest of souls.

God calls each of us to fulfil both roles in our lives today. However, our vocational roles often create a division that is misunderstood by both workplace Christians and pastors. These misunderstandings have led to a weakened and less effective Church.

Pastors have been guilty of viewing their workplace Christians as dollar signs. They sometimes see them for what they can contribute to their ministries instead of equipping them to use their gifts and talents to impact the workplace believer's mission field their workplace.

Workplace Christians have tried to get pastors to operate their churches like businesses, and have used their worldly ways for spiritual purposes. They often view the pastor as the primary ministry worker instead of taking on the responsibility themselves to do the work of the ministry.

This is a grievous sin that exists in the Body of Christ, and it requires repentance from both groups. Unless we recognize this, we will never see the reality of revival that God wants to bring to the business community, and pastors will fail to gain an ally to fully complete the work of the Church in their community.

Are you a pastor who has failed to see the calling that workplace Christians have received to the workplace? If so, ask God to forgive you for viewing your workplace Christians as those to be used for your own purposes.

Are you a workplace believer who sees your church as another business to be run based on worldly measurements? Do you see the pastor's role as one who is primarily responsible for the work of the ministry? If so, you must repent and ask God to forgive you of this unbiblical view.

God has called both of you to fulfil His purposes together through your gifts and talents.

JESUS, THE ETERNAL KING AND PRIEST (14)

Jesus is a king. He was born a king (Matthew 2:2), died as a king (Mark 15:32), and now reigns as the King of kings and Lord of lords (1 Timothy 6:15; Revelation 19:16).

Jesus is also a priest. The office of the true priesthood was found in Jesus Christ. Unlike other high priests who entered the Holy of Holies with the blood of goats and calves, Jesus served as High Priest by offering Himself as a sacrifice once for all.

> *But Christ came as High Priest of the good things to come, with the greater and more perfect tabernacle not made with hands, that is, not of this creation. Not with the blood of goats and calves, but with His own blood He entered the Most Holy Place once for all, having obtained eternal redemption.*
>
> (Hebrews 9:11-12)

He functions as a King and Priest (Hebrews 5:6; 7:1; Revelation 11:15), enabling us to become heirs of His Kingdom which He has established through His sacrificial death on the cross.

> *But God, who is rich in mercy, because of His great love with which He loved us, even when we were dead in trespasses, made us alive together with Christ (by grace you have been saved), and raised us up together, and made us sit together in the heavenly places in Christ Jesus, that in the ages to come He might show the exceeding riches of His grace in His kindness toward us in*

Christ Jesus.

(Ephesians 2:4-7)

Because of His great love and exceeding riches of His grace, He has made us sit together with Him as kings and priests in heavenly places.

In John 1, Jesus was the Word Who created all things! All things were made through Him, and without Him, nothing was made that was made. In Genesis 1, we find that Jesus was working, having many kingly and priestly duties to fulfil. He is the:

Chief Designer & Planner as He designed the universe.
Chief Surveyor as He surveyed the heavens and the earth.
Chief Creative Director as He created the universe.
Chief Architect as He built heaven and earth.
Chief Landscaper as He mapped out the lands and seas.
Chief Space Commander as He created the sun, moon and stars.
Chief Zoologist as He created the animals.
Chief of Oceanography as He created the sea creatures and living things.
Chief of Cattle and Land as He created the lambs, cows and goats.
Chief Gardener as He created the trees and the plants.
Chief Quality Controller as He monitored the various stages of creation-
And so on.

He worked for 6 days and rested on the 7th. And He is an awesome Worker. What did He do on the 7th day? Do nothing? Resting is not doing nothing.

Kings and Priests

And on the seventh day God ended His work which He had done, and He rested on the seventh day from all His work which He had done. Then God blessed the seventh day and sanctified it, because in it He rested from all His work which God had created and made.

(Genesis 2:2-3)

After finishing all His works, He began to reflect and take pleasure admiring and enjoying them on the 7th day. He rejoiced over His creation with joy and singing, blessing and sanctifying each of them! His works are holy and perfect! Yes, work is sacred in the eyes of God. He blessed the seventh day and sanctified it. He did the work of the High Priest, blessing and sanctifying the whole creation.

We need to learn from Jesus how to bless and sanctify the works that we have done! How to rest and be still and enjoy God and His creation!

> Jesus did not only teach in the synagogues and temple, He also ministered in the marketplace

As a king and priest, Jesus modelled love and servanthood in the marketplace. His ministry was also there.

Jesus did not only teach in the synagogues and temple, but He also ministered in the marketplace! Of the 132 public appearances of Jesus in the four gospels, 122 (92%) were in the marketplace. Of the 52 parables He told, 45 (87%) had a

185

> When we genuinely take an interest in the life of the people in our workplace and serve them, we will begin to minister as a king and priest for God in the marketplace just like Jesus our Lord.

marketplace context. Thirty-nine of the 40 (about 97.5%) divine encounters in the Book of Acts were in the marketplace. Jesus is our best model and example, serving as a King and Priest in the marketplace!

He taught His disciples that serving others was essential and effective in winning them to God, and servanthood was the key for true leadership and kingship.

> *But Jesus called them to Himself and said, "You know that the rulers of the Gentiles lord it over them, and those who are great exercise authority over them. Yet it shall not be so among you; but whoever desires to become great among you, let him be your servant. And whoever desires to be first among you, let him be your slave. Just as the Son of Man did not come to be served, but to serve, and to give His life a ransom for many."*
>
> (Matthew 20:25-28)

People do not care what we know; they want to know that we care. When we genuinely take an interest in the life of the people in our workplace and serve them, we will begin to minister as a king and priest for God in the marketplace just like Jesus our Lord.

Our Roles as Kings in the Marketplace
As kings, we need to:
Seek His kingdom and His righteousness.
Do His will.
Do the Father's business His Way.
Be faithful to God.

> *This is a faithful saying: For if we died with Him, we shall also live with Him. If we endure, we shall also reign with Him. If we deny Him, He also will deny us. If we are faithless, He remains faithful; He cannot deny Himself.*
>
> (2 Timothy 2:11-13)

> *Righteousness exalts a nation, but sin is a reproach to any people.*
>
> (Proverbs 14:34)

> *To do righteousness and justice is more acceptable to the LORD than sacrifice.*
>
> (Proverbs 21:3)

> *Take away the wicked from before the king, and his throne will be established in righteousness.*
>
> (Proverbs 25:5)

What we need to know about the Commandments of God, is that they can build and transform nations and turn the hearts of the people back to God. They are also wisdom and understanding to the peoples. They are also righteousness in the sight of God. Where did the British and Americans get their legal laws from? From the Bible! But the moment they turned away from those laws, they moved into darkness and unrighteousness.

> *Therefore be careful to observe them; for this is your wisdom and your understanding in the sight of the peoples who will hear all these statutes, and say, 'Surely this great nation is a wise and understanding people.' "For what great nation is there that has God so near to it, as the LORD our God is to us, for whatever reason we may call upon Him? And what great nation is there that has such statutes and righteous judgments as are in all this law which I set before you this day?* (Deuteronomy 4:6-8).

What is righteousness before God?

> *And the LORD commanded us to observe all these statutes, to fear the LORD our God, for our good always, that He might preserve us alive, as it is this day. Then it will be righteousness for us, if we are careful to observe all these commandments before the LORD our God, as He has commanded us.'*
>
> (Deuteronomy 6:24-25)

> *Blessed are those who do His commandments that they may have the right to the tree of life, and may enter through the gates into the city.*
>
> (Revelation 22:14)

Our Roles as Priests in the Marketplace

As priests, we need to:

> Present our bodies as a living sacrifice, holy, acceptable to God,

which is our reasonable service. Be transformed by the renewing of our mind, not conforming to the world, so that we may prove what is that good and acceptable and perfect will of God.

(Romans 12:2)

Continually offer the sacrifice of praise to God, that is, the fruit of our lips, giving thanks to His name. Do good and share with others, for with such sacrifices God is well pleased.

(Hebrews 13:15 – 16)

Many Christians think that today, "kings" refers to the laymen, businessmen, and bankers, and "priests" refers to fulltime and pastoral staff in the church. But this is not true. Their definition is wrong! This is the Greek mindset, stating that the kings are secular but the priests are sacred; if you are doing Christian ministry or mission work, you are a sacred or full-time Christian. If you are not, then you are secular.

The Hebraic mindset is different. Regardless of their occupations, all Jews are to worship God and obey His commandments. Godly Jews believe in the Lord and obey His commandments, and secular Jews simply don't.

> Jesus is our best model and example, serving as a King and Priest in the marketplace

The line between sacred and secular Christians should also be the same. The dividing factors should be between holiness and unholiness; righteousness and unrighteousness; kingdom and non-kingdom.

All Christians have the same Bible as their Christian leaders working in churches; not one verse more or one commandment less. We are to worship God and obey Him regardless of race, language or occupation.

A Christian working in a church or ministry can be in a spiritual place and yet do unspiritual tasks. They can be unrighteous and unholy before the Lord. A very good example is that of the sons of Eli (1 Sam. 2:22-25). They were the priests in the Temple. Besides other bad reports, they were seducing the young women who assisted at the entrance of the Tabernacle. They despised the Lord and were killed by Him.

> We are to worship God and obey Him regardless of race, language or occupation

But a Christian businessman or a working professional can be in a secular place and yet do spiritual tasks. They can be righteous and holy before the Lord, doing business God's way. Abraham was a businessman, very rich in livestock, silver and gold (Gen. 13:1-5). He was very wealthy, with sheep and cattle and many servants. In the eyes of God, Abraham was righteous on the basis that he believed God.

Another case was King David. He reigned for 40 years. Yet God said that David was a man after His own heart, and he did everything that God wanted him to do (Acts 13:22).

Joseph was a Prime Minister serving Pharaoh. He was serving the Lord full-time in the Egyptian palace. Daniel was serving the Lord full-time in the Babylonian palace. Joseph and Daniel were effectively doing what the Lord had called them to do. Nothing short of His glory!

God is omnipresent. To say that God only works in the churches and Christian organisations is boxing God up and limiting His authority. The earth belongs to God! Everything on the earth is His! (Psalm 24:1). God cannot be boxed. Very often, God speaks outside His Temple!

Jesus chose His disciples from the marketplace. Andrew, Peter, James and John were fishermen (Mark 1:16-19). Matthew was a tax collector (Matt. 9:9). None of His twelve was from the Temple or the synagogues. They were ordinary people having secular occupations. Jesus is still calling men and women in the marketplace to become His disciples. He desires to build His Kingdom of love among the peoples.

THE MARKETPLACE IS A SPIRITUAL PLACE

We need to understand that our calling and training is to fulfil God's purposes in the marketplace. We are coming to a place where there is intense spiritual warfare going on all the time…

> We need to understand that our calling and training is to fulfil God's purposes in the marketplace.

a place where demonic forces and principalities abound and reside. Many of the idols, altars and high places of the pagan gods are there.

We need to be the kings and priests in the marketplace, taking our places in spiritual battles and restoring righteousness and holiness, building His Kingdom of love!

> *And He Himself gave some to be apostles, some prophets, some evangelists, and some pastors and teachers, for the equipping of the saints for the work of ministry, for the edifying of the body of Christ, till we all come to the unity of the faith and of the knowledge of the Son of God, to a perfect man, to the measure of the stature of the fullness of Christ;*
>
> (Ephesians 4:11-13)

The aim of the fivefold ministry is to equip the saints for the work of the ministry.

What's the work of the ministry? The Greek word is *"diakonia"* which means every labour, service or business that benefits others. This work of the ministry is basically to serve God and the peoples in every business or service that benefits others. A teacher teaches, a fisherman fishes, a farmer farms and a pastor pastors, and so on.

The governments of the nations have it correct by naming their ministries:
Ministry of Defence.
Ministry of Education.

Kings and Priests

Ministry of Finance.
Ministry of Foreign Affairs.
Ministry of Health.
Ministry of Home Affairs.
Ministry of Manpower.
Ministry of the Environment.
Ministry of Trade and Industry.
Many of these ministries draw their wisdom and knowledge from the 613 laws of God!

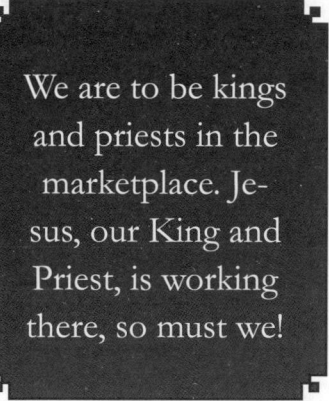

We are to be kings and priests in the marketplace. Jesus, our King and Priest, is working there, so must we!

This is all about seeking God's kingdom and His righteousness.

God's Kingdom consists of:
- A King - who rules and reigns in righteousness
- Law and order - His precepts and statutes about the economy, trades and businesses.
- Public Services - for education, development, defence, finance, health, etc.
- A Temple - a place of worship and adoration.

God is working in the temple and also in the marketplace. We need to serve one another as the Body of Christ, esteeming others better than ourselves. We must not commit the same errors and mistakes like the Israelites in the past. We are called to be kings and priests in the marketplace. Jesus, our King and Priest, is working there, so must we!

MODERN DAY KINGS (15)

Old Testament kings served two primary roles: to rule over God's people and to wage war against their enemies. They oversaw all commerce, land, trade, and the economy of their nations, always separating a portion of their treasury to the priests. More so, they were NOT allowed to perform "priestly" functions, through the then clear and distinct separation of church and business.

Under the New Covenant, as modern-day kings, we have an expanded role. Not only do we reign over our sphere of marketplace influence, but we also are appointed to serve in a priestly/pastoral role over our tribe.

Characteristics of Modern-day Kings

The modern-day kings:
- Are anointed and called to five of the seven mountains of influence (business, education, media, arts and entertainment, and government).
- Expect great results: expansion, multiplication, exponential growth as he/she sees Kingdom business as supernatural.
- Expand the Kingdom outside the church into the marketplace spheres.
- Are the movers and shakers in the Kingdom.
- Do not leave their work to start ministries but view their jobs/businesses as a sacred part of a King's

destiny.

- Do not bend to culture: they transform it.
- Do not beg: they decree.
- Administer in the Spirit in their marketplace as freely as a Priest in the church.
- Take spiritual authority over their workplace (office, employees, company, customers, industry, etc.).
- Embrace their appointed role within the five-fold ministry at work (walk in the role of apostle, prophet, pastor, teacher or evangelist).
- Unleash the full power of heaven into their market.

MODERN DAY PRIESTS (15)

Old Testament priests exclusively served within the wall of the temple. They seldom stepped into the marketplace except to prophesy or warn/call out the kings of current or potential missteps. Their anointment was for the house of God whereas kings were anointed only for the marketplace... or so conventional "wisdom" had them believe.

Modern-day priests (who nornally consider themselves as full-time pastors) can indeed carry this same anointment for the house of God and also play a critical role in the marketplace, creating impact in companies and organisations.

Characteristics of Modern-Day Priests

The modern-day priest anointment includes:
- A clear, distinctive calling within Faith/Religion Mountain to build the church.
- Grow a strong five-fold leadership ministry within their body.
- Equip and grow the spiritual foundation and strength of their tribe.
- Walk by the side of their kingdom members as spiritual advisers and sherpherds.
- Provide their kings with an apostolic covering for their marketplace mission.
- Equip their kings to serve in the role of both a king and priest in their work.
- Sever the traditional divisions of "clergy vs. lay leaders" while raising an army of Spirit-led, Kingdom-focused warriors to invade and conquer their marketplace mountains.
- Embrace their marketplace kings as far more than an instant cash machine but as a strategic partner in transforming the world for the Kingdom of God.

YOUR CHALLENGE

One person; two roles.

You ARE ABLE…and should…walk in both roles within your sphere of influence. If you are not currently walking in the role of both a leader and a spiritual guide to those around you, you may be missing your marketplace calling.

For you have the power of the Kingdom within you (Ephesians 3:20). And for many of your colleagues, your supernatural Kingdom power is the ONLY Kingdom power they may have, speaking into their lives.

Be bold and walk, in both your King and Priest anointing.

CHAPTER SUMMARY

1. **The Role of Priest and King**
   a. Separate Roles in the Old Testament.
   b. Combined Roles in the New Testament.

2. **Jesus, the Eternal King and Priest**
   a. Jesus is our best model and example, serving as a King and Priest in the marketplace!

3. **Our Roles as Kings in the Marketplace**
   a. As kings, we need to:
   i. Seek His kingdom and His righteousness.
   ii. Do His will.
   iii. Do the Father's business His Way.
   iv. Be faithful to God.

4. **Our Roles as Priests in the Marketplace**
   a. As priests, we need to:
   i. Present our bodies as a living sacrifice, holy, acceptable to God, which is our reasonable service. Be transformed by the renewing of our mind, not conforming to the world, so that we may prove what is that good and acceptable and perfect will of God. (Romans 12:2)
   ii. Continually offer the sacrifice of praise to God, that is, the fruit of our lips, giving thanks to Hiname. Do good and share with others, for with such sacrifices God is well pleased. (Hebrews 13:15 – 16)

ENDNOTES

Chapter One:
1. Luke 5:30 TPT
2. Mark 1:14-15 KJV

Chapter Two:
1. Matthew 6:10 NASB
2. Mathew 5:3 KJV
3. Matthew 6:9-10 KJV
4. Matthew 12:28 KJV
5. Mark 1:14-15 ESV
6. Matthew 16:19-19 MSG
7. Mark 1:15 NIV
8. John 3:5 ESV
9. Romans 14:17-18 NASB
10. Matthew 6:33 NASB

Chapter Three:
1. Romans 13:3-4 NASB
2. Ephesians 4:11-12
3. 1 Corinthians 10:31
4. Colossians 3:17; 23-24
5. Corinthians 10:31
6. Colossians 3:17,23

7. Philippians 2:6-8

8. 2 Corinthians 2:15-16; 3:5-6

9. Ecclesiastes 2:20-23

10. Galatians 5:18

11. Matthew 6:9-10

12. Mark 16:17-18

13. Romans 15:18-19

Chapter Four:

1. Colossians 3:23 TPT

2. Colossians 3:23-24

3. Proverbs 11:1

4. Psalms 15:1-3

5. 1 Peter 3:15 ESV

6. Proverbs 22:29

7. Genesis 4:25

Chapter Five:

1. Luke 4:6 The Voice

2. Matthew 22:37,39

3. Joshua 3:10

4. Deuteronomy 7:1

Chapter Six:

1. Matthew 16:18 TPT

2. Matthew 16:18 MSG

Chapter Seven:
1. Revelation 5:10 KJV
2. Hebrews 9:11-12
3. Ephesians 2:4-7
4. Psalm 75:6-7
5. Genesis 1:1-2
6. Genesis 2:2-3
7. Matthew 20:25-28
8. 2 Timothy 2:11-13
9. Proverbs 14:34
10. Proverbs 21:3
11. Proverbs 25:5
12. Deuteronomy 4:6-8
13. Deuteronomy 6:24-25
14. Revelation 22:14
15. Romans 12:1-2
16. Hebrews 13:16-16
17. Ephesians 4:11-13

BIBLIOGRAPHY

1. **Colson, Chuck.** How Shall We Then Live? Carol Stream : Tyndall House Publishers,, 1999.

2. **Munroe, Myles.** Kingdom Principles. s.l. : Destiny Image Publishers.

3. **Mattera, Joseph.** Contrasting a Kingdom Mindset with a Church Mindset. Patheos. [Online] 11 November 2010. [Cited: 17 April 2019.]

4. **Bible.org.** Expanding Your Concept of Ministry. Bible.org. [Online] [Cited: 1 May 2019.] https://bible.org/seriespage/session-1-expanding-your-concept-ministry.

5. **Hilman, Os.** Four Types of Christians in the Workplace. Transform Work UK. [Online] Transform Work UK. [Cited: 20 May 2019.] http://transformworkuk.org/Articles/300734/Transform_Work_UK/Old_Folders_and/Resources_Individuals/Workplace_Hot_Topics/Faith_and_Work/Four_Types_of.aspx.

6. **Greear, J.D.** Work as Worship. 2014.

7. Vallotton, Kris. Kris Vallotton Ministries. Facebook. [Online] 30 April 2019. https://www.facebook.com/kvministries/posts/theres-so-much-confusion-over-something-called-the-seven-mountain-mandate-often-/10156432327803741/.

8. **Hugh, Whelchel.** What is the Mission of God's People. Institute for Faith, Work & Economics. [Online] Institute for Faith, Work & Economics, 4 May 2015. [Cited: 30 May 2019.] https://tifwe.org/the-mission-of-gods-people-is-found-in-the-cultural-mandate/.

9. **Sorrell, Will.** The Cultural Mandate and the Great Commission: The Power of Integration. Business as Mission - BAM. [Online] 30 October 2018. http://businessasmission.com/the-cultural-mandate-and-the-great-commission/.

10. **Enlow, Johnny.** The Seven Mountain Prophecy. Lake Mary, Florida : Creation House, 2008. 978-1-59979-287-3.

11. **Mattera, Joseph.** 20 Contrasts Between the Box Church and the Kingdom-Centred Church. Charisma News. [Online] 10 October 2014. [Cited: 19 April 2019.] https://www.charismanews.com/opinion/the-pulse/45967-20-contrasts-between-the-box-church-and-the-kingdom-centered-church.

12. **Hemphill, Kenneth S**. Beyond Church Growth: Kingdom Expansion. Baptist Press. [Online] Southern Baptist Convention - SBC LIFE, 1 January 2006. [Cited: 2 May 2019.] http://www.sbclife.net/article/1336/beyond-church-growth-kingdom-expansion.

13. **Hilman, Os.** Kings and Priests. Marketplace Leaders. [Online] 27 December 2016. http://www.marketplaceleaders.org/kings-and-priests/#ixzz5ntaDsGRx.

14. Kings And Priests In the Marketplace. The Josh Link. [Online] 3 August 2010. https://www.thejoshlink.com/article263.htm.

15. Harris, Dr Jim. You are a King and a Priest. The Kingdom Institute. [Online] https://thekingdominstitute.org/articles/you-are-a-king-and-a-priest/.

WHERE IT ALL BEGINS

SOME new friends of mine reading this book may have no idea how to get started with life in (with) Jesus and walking with Him to extend His Kingdom. Let me take a moment to explain where to begin.

The Bible makes it clear that all of us need a Saviour someone to pay for our sins. We have all sinned and fall short of God's glory. Without recognizing the Saviour and accepting the sarifice He made for us, and the price He paid, we are disconnected from Him and consequently live a life of bondage and torment, chasing hopeless dreams.

Jesus died on the Cross for us and He also died as us. He took the penalty for every wrong that we will ever do. Jesus wants to do more than forgive us. He wants to give us a brand-new life in the Kingdom of God right now on this earth. He also desires for us to enter Heaven when we pass from this life into the next.

As if this isn't enough, He has promised that when we ask Him into our hearts, we will become "born again" and become new creations. He gives us a new life, a new heart and a new mind.

You have read about advancing God's Kingdom in this book and may be asking right now, "What do I have to do to begin this amazing Kingdom life?" Good question!

You need to be willing to give the leadership role of your life to Jesus and be serious about following Him. You need to acknowledge that you have sinned and are separated from Him and that you need His help to change. You need to ask Him to forgive you, and you need to forgive everyone who has hurt you.

If you are willing to do these things, if you are willing to follow Jesus, please pray this prayer:

Lord Jesus, I have done many wrong things in my life and need You to forgive me. I am sorry for living my life without You in my heart: the dreams I have pursued without You leading me. From now on, I want to follow you and let you be in charge of my entire life. I am ready to forsake my old life and take on Your life, Your ways and Your desires. I forgive everyone who has harmed or hurt me in any way and I permit them right now to live, free from my revenge. I ask You to send Your Holy Spirit into my life and baptize me with Your love and power. Amen!

Now find a good church where you can grow spiritually and go there as often as possible. Look for someone mature in Christ to mentor you: sometimes this happens naturally by being part of fellowship groups in a church. Read your Bible daily (begin with the Book of John) and ask the Holy Spirit to teach you as you read. Take time to pray every day, listening for Jesus to speak to you as you seek Him. Lastly, share your life and faith with others.

May the King of Glory meet you in the palace of your dreams as you begin your new life in the Kingdom of God!
Love,
Silas A. Achu,
Bethel Atlanta Cameroon
Buea – Cameroon.
www.bethelatlantaafrica.com

ABOUT THE AUTHOR

SILAS A. Achu is a pastor, trainer, and leadership coach. Silas has a passion for Christians in the workplace: equipping them to become effective ministers and leaders in their spheres of influence in the marketplace.

He is the Founding Director of Lead from the Heart, a life-purpose coaching & leadership development organization. Together with his wife, Vivian A. Achu, they both serve as Relationship & Marriage Counsellors where they train, counsel & coach people to build healthy relationships and strong marriages.

You can contact him via email at silasachu@outlook.com or via telephone at +237 670 440 183.

You can discover more about Silas on his websites: www.leadfromtheheart.org & www.silasachu.com

You can purchase additional copies of this book
and other book titles by the author.
Call: (+237) 670 440 183 | 696 609 919
Email: silasachu@outlook.com
Or visit www.silasachu.com

OTHER BOOKS BY SILAS A. ACHU

Dreams to Reality – Discover the Secrets to Fulfilling Your Destiny | **1st Edition 2016**

Dreams to Reality – Discover the Secrets to Fulfilling Your Destiny | **2nd Edition Revised & Updated**